Questions
on the Quest

Questions
on the Quest

SEARCH AND DISCOVERY IN THE WORLD WITHIN,
THE WORLD AROUND, AND WORLDS BEYOND

MARCUS BACH

Published in San Francisco by Harper & Row, Publishers

NEW YORK, HAGERSTOWN, SAN FRANCISCO, LONDON

FIRST EDITION

Designed by Jim Mennick

Library of Congress Cataloging in Publication Data

Bach, Marcus, 1906–
   QUESTIONS ON THE QUEST.

   1. Spiritual life—Addresses, essays, lectures.
2. Conduct of life—Addresses, essays, lectures.
3. Religion—Addresses, essays, lectures. I. Title.
BL624.B28 1978   248   77-20464
ISBN 0-06-060320-8

Contents

~~~~~~

Before the Beginning

The question mark (?) is a serpent, an ancient symbol of wisdom, standing on its tail. Properly understood, it is also the sign of how knowledge has come into being.

By way of endless questions and answers, I have challenged the serpent and occasionally persuaded it to stand upright as if registering amazement or righteous indignation, causing it to assume a form like this!. More often, however, it simply curled up at the end of an answer and lay there, a motionless dot, or period biding its time. I have also seen it slither away from convincing encounters leaving nothing more than a broken trail – – – –.

This mythology about serpent-wisdom-power goes far back in time, back to Eden, in fact, when the snake slyly planted a question in the mind of Eve: if she and Adam ate of the fruit of the tree of knowledge would they lose their lease on paradise? With provocative cunning the serpent found its niche in religious lore wherever anyone had a will to believe or a wish to doubt.

The opinion persists that the snake is evil, but how can that be when God said that everything He made was good? If the old reptile is all bad, why did Jesus tell his disciples to be as wise as serpents?

The answer seems to be that evil is of the mind and that the serpent, as a token of wisdom and a sign of honest questioning, tempts us toward an ever deeper understanding of ourselves. For we learn and grow through persistent inquiry into things, separating truth from error by our questions on the quest. Make no mistake, God was in the snake!

Today the serpent's slithering trail, marked by questions not fully answered and often distorted by the past, is leading us more and more into the inward, personalized journey. The quest is for an integrated ordered life, physically fit, mentally alert, and spiritually fulfilling.

Today our exploration includes the mystical, the occult, the hidden, no less than the scientific, the material, the holistic. Most of us believe we carry answers semi-consciously within ourselves, or we would never have asked the questions in the first place. Truth is where we find it.

There are those, of course, who insist that the only real answer to life's persistent quest is found not in following the serpent's trail of search and discovery, but in the symbol of the circle O, that is, the snake eating its tail.

In this circle concept, we are told, lies the answer to the positive-negative linking of the circuit of cosmic life, and we are urged to get into the center of it simply by a leap of faith. The popularity of the Tao, the mandala, the karmic wheel, the hoop, the loop, the cosmic egg, has become a graphic reminder of the ultimate goal: nirvana, salvation, celestial peace, an unquestioning world.

Fair enough. But a snake eating its tail may also be a sign of frustration as well as an easy way out, and there are those of us who would rather keep on going straight along the trail, meeting our doubts and challenges face to face, rather than get hooked by a journey round and round.

The question remains: which is the better way? One answer is: make it an adventure, think straight, and learn to live with ambiguity. For the true secret of the quest is found in the questing, as true love is found in loving, joy in being joyful, and peace in living peacefully. Let's never lose the lure of life, for nothing of the good that we have found by honest searching is ever lost.

The reason people send their questions to me is simply because they want a companion when they are confronted by interrogation points in their inward, onward-going search. They are lonely, and I, at times, am lonely, too. They are ferreting out elusive truths and so am I. Here they are—here we are—trying to find our way, and what we want and need is someone with opinions but not stubborn opinionation, answers but no illusions of infallibility, analysis without intimidation, and hopefully someone who has a light touch while focusing on problems that often seem perplexingly dark.

Most people who write to me do not know me, but they know that I know something about the nature of the serpent. How do they know? They just know. And I know. And together we recognize the trail for what it is.

But what is it? What is this interrogation point, snakelike in the shadows? What mood is it in? What does it have in mind? What is it trying to teach us? These are the real questions. Is it a hissing antagonist showing a forked tongue and poised for attack, or is it a friend in disguise, a decoy without venom? Or could it be a worldly wise, divinely appointed guardian of a wisdom tree ripe with answers if we but have the courage and the reach of mind to gather knowledge under its branches in the center of the Garden?

From my earliest research among religious and cultural groups around the world, a work which began with my book, *They Have Found A Faith* (Bobbs-Merrill, Inc., New York), I realized from readers' letters that church leaders generally lagged behind their parishioners in curiosity and interest in the lives and worship of people of other religions and races. The real, live interest and empathy came from people in the pews and from non-churchgoers. They were the ones who had the questing spirit and the questions, and they were window-shopping among new religions which had once been branded as sects and cults. But for fear of being turned off, they were reluctant to share their inquisitiveness with the clergy or with other professionals who had never taken time to get person-to-person information from primary sources.

As my later books appeared,*my mail carrier was among the first to know something was happening. So was I.

Inquiries about religion's role in health and healing, interest in occultism, and parapsychological phenomena, as well as the emergence of "little-known" groups elbowing their way into church street

---

* *Faith And My Friends,* (Bobbs-Merrill, Inc., New York), *The Circle of Faith,* (Hawthorn Books, Inc., New York), *God and the Soviets,* (Thomas Y. Crowell Co., New York), *Had You Been Born In Another Faith,* (Prentice-Hall, Inc., Englewood Cliffs, NJ) *Strange Sects and Curious Cults,* (Dodd, Mead & Co., New York), *Strangers At The Door, Major Religions of the World,* (Abingdon Press, Nashville).

left no doubt that the winds of change were blowing and that traditional denominations no longer provided a total shelter for those in search of meaningful answers.

The real breakthrough came with the rapidly expanding metaphysical groups such as the Unity movement, Science of Mind, Divine Science, the International New Thought Alliance and the like. From their inception they insisted that life was an experience to be enjoyed, that the solution to personal problems was simply a matter of finding the key to Self, that health, prosperity and inner peace rather than sin and suffering were what the world's great spiritual teachers, Jesus in particular, had in mind.

The letters that inundated me were proof that a new adventure in faith had taken hold of the laity and was moving through society at large, from young people unbound by the religious hardware of the past to church devotees who felt it was time to follow the interrogation point wherever it might lead.

In the spring of 1972 I stopped in at the Unity headquarters in Unity Village, Missouri, to share my findings with Jim Decker, editor of *Unity* magazine. Jim knew about my work. I knew about Unity. During my early research I had authored *The Unity Way of Life* (Prentice-Hall, Inc., Englewood Cliffs, NJ), a book subsequently reprinted in continuing editions by the Unity Press. Jim assured me that my answer to the question, "What is the Unity movement?" still stood as I had reported it in the book:

> The Unity School of Christianity is a spiritual movement without any preoccupation about getting converts. It is a religious-educational movement teaching the use of God-consciousness in everyday life, clarifying the working of divine law, explaining the action of the mind which it calls the connecting link between God and man.

Unity had grown phenomenally. It now had its own post office, training school, acres of orchards, offices, motels, retreat grounds, chapel, prayer tower, a meatless cafeteria, a huge printing plant, at Unity Village just a prayer away from Kansas City where the movement was founded by Charles and Myrtle Fillmore in 1889. The philosophy of this husband-wife team now spanned the world with its teachings. Unity churches had given the movement the status of a religious denomination and much of the spiritual power was generated at the Village by Silent Unity, a prayer service functioning day and night, annually answering millions of calls and sending out endless affirmations to people in need.

Taking note of the batches of letters I spread out on his orderly desk, editor Jim Decker decided to recommend that *Questions on the Quest* be given a trial run in *Unity* magazine. Its introduction in the June 1972 issue was an immediate success and it became an uninterrupted feature. With the coming of a new editor, Tom Witherspoon, in 1977 the column was expanded. Now, with this Harper & Row publication, *Questions on the Quest* is launched into the book trade, while letters continue to increase in number and in their range of interest.

Here is a search for understanding of life, death, visions, truth, love, karma, reincarnation, sex, marriage, psychism, longevity, heaven, hell, sin and salvation, war and peace, pain and passion, God and His special agents—all of which were part of the quest when I was vagabonding around the world with religion as my beat as it is today.

As questions take new forms, we should trust the interrogation point and let things happen rather than try to make them happen, recognizing that life reveals its meaning as the restlessly moving question mark lures us on.

Today there is no significant difference between the quest of churchgoers and the quest of those who worship and believe without the benefit of clergy. Always, as there are questions that prompt answers, so there are answers which lead to further questioning and to the blazing of fresh trails of thought. And always there are those who tell me they already knew what I tell them, but that they hadn't known they knew until they were told.

So, knowing what we know, let's walk together through the pages of a book which is as much yours as mine. Let's meet the so-called serpent whatever its mood or wherever it may lead. If you have further questions, write me, and if you have better answers, let me know.

MARCUS BACH

1

Of Self-Discovery and Self-Esteem

~~~~~~~~~~~~~~~~~~~~~~~~~~~~~~~~~~~

Question: What is a neurotic? A friend (perhaps acquaintance would be more correct) once told me that I was neurotic. I laughed it off, but inwardly I have never forgotten the incident and must admit it troubles me.

A. E.

Answer: Neurotic traits are those seemingly unconscious habits or deep-seated tendencies that prevent us from being our true, highest, most integrated selves. No doubt we are all a bit neurotic, just as we are all a bit unique.

There are degrees of neuroses, just as there are degrees of functional nervous disorders. If your friend has a compulsion to label others as neurotic, he or she is fully as "neurotic" as they are. Laugh it off once more, this time for *good!* Rest easy in your own secure opinion of yourself. Develop self-esteem through a consciousness of your inner strength and faith.

MB

Question: Can human nature be changed? Sometimes I wonder.

J. B. J.

Answer: If it can't, we've had it. The teachings of all great prophets, seers and avatars insist that human nature is ever fluid, expanding, unfolding, and susceptible to unlimited growth. All we need are convincing *changers* to quietly assist in the changing. Why not be one?

MB

Question: I have been praying for twenty months for peace of mind. I was married for twenty-five years when my husband decided to leave me. I love him dearly and I know that there is no return.

At first, I did everything I could to hurt him back. This action has caused my work to suffer. My job is no longer secure. I pray for him now and am able to accept our separation, but I cannot get him out of my mind and perform my job as I did before. I think of him and repeat over and over, "God's love fills your soul." However, I need more help.

I have hobbies, but somehow they are not enough. I read the Bible, but I just cannot grasp the full effects because my mind is always racing toward the great hurt I have. When I see our children and grandchildren they are reminders. I cannot get my mind off him. Can you help?

E. E.

Answer: Sometimes our forced attempts at forgetting and forgiving are actually unconscious efforts to remember and condemn, so subtle is the working of the mind. Compulsive prayers may also be means to harbor resentment, rather than channels open to release it.

Take a good look at yourself and try to analyze your deepest motivations. This is the level that you must work on. Hobbies, reading the Bible, getting away from it all, only compound the situation if they make you want to cling to someone whom you should now willingly "loose and let go." If all your attention is focused on building an external world out of harmony with your internal intentions, you are on a false trail.

I have a strong feeling, however, that you are confronted by, and ready to take advantage of, a tremendous opportunity for spiritual growth and fulfillment. Let your husband go so that he can grow, and you will grow in the process.

Here's a tip, strange and simple though it seems: if you walk straighter, breathe deeper, visualize your better self, look and be your best and feel the power and strength of God more perfectly, you will find your capacity for peace of mind immeasurably and immediately improved. Try it!

MB

Question: I am coming to you with a question that I have been struggling with for some time. What is your explanation for these instant "Jesus conversions" that we are inundated with, such as those of Charles Colson and other prominent individuals?

I have suffered a series of family tragedies for many years and have searched and prayed and bled, trying to find spiritual sustenance, yet here are all these people, many of whom have never even thought in spiritual terms, suddenly "taking Jesus as my personal Savior" (a term repugnant to me), and suddenly their lives are marvelous and they are living on a cloud. I shall be most grateful if you will comment on this.

J.

Answer: In my study of world religions, no phenomenon is more graphic than the "instant conversion" to which you refer. I doubt whether it is actually "instant," however, because unseen lines of influence have been woven through the years. It is only the culmination that we term instantaneous. Whatever the time scale may be, this transformation, which takes place when a seeker suddenly identifies with the symbol of the power sought, is always dramatic and arresting.

This miraculous change in life is by no means confined to seekers of Christ. It is found in dedication to Buddha, to Krishna, to Mohammed, to rabbis, avatars, prophets, seers and gurus, ancient and modern. It is as universal as love and as inexplicable.

Though some people seem to "convert" more easily than others, nearly everyone, even the most reserved and rational, has a longing for identification with a higher power and a need for something to live *by,* that becomes more viable and supportive when related to someone to live *for.*

In all the world, no personality so dramatically symbolizes the personification of God as does Jesus Christ. The name is magical and the power, supreme. Although Christianity is a minority religion, Jesus is a major figure when viewed in the light of "conversion," or what I term "transformation by attachment."

In a world that is often overwhelming to us, Jesus assures us that He has overcome the world. In a society where the trick has been to "get by with it" if you can, He seems to say that one can never really get by with anything. At a time when the tendency seems to be toward covering up or copping out, He is the unrelenting advocate of personal responsibility. These powers of Christ have made an impact bordering on something quite mystical, certainly on a mystique.

I know young people, Jesus people and self-styled Jesus Freaks, who have kicked heroin without withdrawal symptoms because they had been "converted" under the power of the Holy Spirit. I have witnessed instantaneous life changes under the impact of the so-called "Baptism of the Holy Ghost." This is not mere posturing, but, to many, a real and sincere spiritual rebirth.

"Take Jesus as my personal Savior" is the typical slogan, the classic cliché of the ardent convert to Christ. As real, and, to many, as annoying, as the slogans "washed by the blood" or "saved by His grace," it is nonetheless part of the mystique. Do not be concerned if you are turned off by those who follow this path. There is a way for them, and there is a way for you.

It was not an "instant conversion" for Charles Colson. Out of a deep disillusionment and a shattered idealism he turned, as many others have, to the Christ within—the recognition of his own divine nature, the same nature as that made manifest in the historical Jesus.

Colson was aided in attaining this awareness by Senator Harold Hughes and others in Washington who have kept spiritual vigil through personal dedication and prayer group participation. Conversion is often forged in personal struggle, fashioned by conflicting circumstances, and if there is the momentary ecstasy of "living on a cloud," there may also have been the agony of some very earthy experiences such as the tragedies you have suffered through.

Let's have the will to believe that true searching and sincere prayer pay off in their own way, in their own time, and that the odyssey of life—whether Colson's or yours or mine or anyone's—is ever in the process of spiritual unfoldment and growth.

MB

Question: Eleven years ago I had what is called a breakdown. One of the symptoms was that awful, destructive thoughts would constantly come into my mind, and I had the fear that they would happen. I spent the majority of my energy trying to fight them, which only made it worse.

I went to a prominent psychiatrist and paid a good amount for help with this problem. His advice to me was, "When these thoughts come, go along with them and try even harder to make the bad things happen." His theory was that when I realized the things did not happen, I would know that the thoughts were harmless and would be cured of my distress.

Unfortunately, when I followed his advice some very disastrous things did happen. As you can guess, I have been living in a state of fear and guilt ever since.

Can I really cause something bad to happen to someone? I don't want to believe it. I keep hoping that maybe there was some other explanation. I felt guided to write to you, for I know you will tell me the truth. If it was my fault, maybe there is some way I can make up for it and find a degree of peace.

P. C. R.

Answer: You have left an alluring gap in your story. What did the psychiatrist say when you reported the disastrous things that happened? But, for our purpose, no matter. Go on from here and, for a change, go with God.

Begin by thinking highly of yourself. You now know that whatever you impress on your subconscious mind expresses itself as a condition or an event. If you have the power to think destructive thoughts, rest assured you have an equal or greater capacity to think constructively and lovingly. This is what the "prominent psychiatrist" should have told you. Thoughts are patterns of energy, and energy is power. It is up to you how you utilize this power. You have it. Use it for good. To assume that compounding and reemphasizing negative thoughts will create positive, constructive actions is contrary to the laws of Truth.

As to the disastrous happenings, I feel that you dipped psychically into the timeless pool of events and foresaw the possibility of the happenings. But there is a difference between foreseeing and foreordaining, though there may be a strong relationship between the two. Circumstances affect mind fully as much as mind affects circumstances.

Yes, begin thinking highly of yourself and your constructive capabilities. Believe that God wants to use your energy and your power for good. Say to your intruding feelings of fear and guilt: "I am stronger than you. I am guarded, guided and governed by the power of almighty God!" Poison your mind no longer by repeating destructive thoughts. Purify your mind by affirming the mind of Christ in you.

You can do it. Do not let anyone throw you off. Eleven years is much too long to bear the burden of a breakdown! Release it. Let it go. The power of God in you is stronger than your psychiatrist's technique. Dwell on inner strength instead of weakness. Claim the truth that the kingdom of God is within you, and have the will to believe that your past experiences will now be utilized for spiritual growth.

MB

Question: For one who does not already have the gift of faith but feels the need for spiritual growth and understanding, what path would you suggest? By this I mean, are there positive ways to increase one's awareness and faith? It is one thing to simply read articles but quite another to actually *feel* this inside, especially if one is prone to intellectualize things. I would really appreciate your assistance.

S. R.

Answer: Your letter reached me at my cabin in Canada. I mention this in order to suggest at least one path by which awareness and faith may be increased: the path of nature, with eyes and ears alert to God's great outdoor. Just to be still for a while, in surroundings where the only sounds you hear are those of Mother Nature and her incredible family, leads to the feeling inside that you mention.

Forgive me for being snoopy, but I checked the population of the town in the Northwest where you live. My atlas gives the population as 1,074. That being the case, you should be able to hear the songs of birds, see the miracle of migratory flights, smell the scent of freshly cut grass and feel the pulse of God in streams and smogless sky. All of these are "paths" that link the environmental world to the world within. Here, in quietude and in meditation are found the seeds of spiritual growth and understanding.

Not that God cannot be found in cities—but that is another matter.

You asked for "positive ways" to increase faith. To keep your heart attuned to nature is definitely one "organic" path to the feeling and the assurance you so earnestly desire.

The true discovery of God is always found in our relatedness to basic things in life. I sense that you already know this, though you may not know that you know it. And isn't this true of most of us who try to intellectualize the gift of faith, rather than simply realizing we already possess it?

MB

Question: It is now believed that we humans have been around for several million years. Sometime around 1500 B.C., the Jews received a set of moral laws in the form of the Ten Commandments. Did older civilizations have such moral laws, or was this something brand new with Moses? If it was something new, how did man behave before that? Man is not inherently good. Did he murder and steal without compunction?

G. C.

Answer: Your categorical statement that "man is not inherently good" must, of course, be balanced by the categorical claim that "man is not inherently evil." In fact, since a tenet of most of the world's religions is that we were made in the image of God, inasmuch as we believe that God is good, we can infer that, from a spiritual point of view, we are basically and inherently not so bad!

True, often when we would do good, evil is present with us, but oftener, when we would do evil, good is even more present. Before the coming of an official "moral law," each person was governed by conscience, an extrasensory source of insight into what is right and wrong for that particular individual. Early religionists described conscience as "the voice of God in the soul."

Various factors entered into the formulation of moral values in society: social customs, divine revelations, the need for survival, dreams, interpretations of natural law and so on. To preserve what were considered constructive values, creeds and legal codes were promulgated and enforced. Behind these codifications lay a spiritual pursuit: an attempt to determine the wish and favor of the gods or God.

Though we believe that Christianity raised individuals to their highest appreciation of moral and ethical principles, pre-Christian religions and philosophies also contained high standards of right and wrong.

Since you indicate an intense interest in this subject, why not spend a day in the public library researching the question? Ask the reference librarian for the Code of Hammurabi, an amazing compilation of laws and precepts purportedly given by divine instruction to the Babylonian king Hammurabi some two thousand years before the coming of Christ. Also, check into Ikhnaton (Amenhotep IV), a king of Egypt who reigned some fifteen hundred years before Jesus' birth. And do not overlook Confucius, Lao-tzu, Buddha, Plato and other forerunners of Jesus who taught that the Spirit of Truth is an infallible guide to human conduct.

The golden thread running through most religions is the conviction that human beings are inherently good and made in the image of God. If this belief still needs proof, the ultimate test is probably ourselves. How we basically feel about ourselves gives us an insight, to a degree at least, as to how others feel about themselves.

MB

Question: I have a confession to make. I am a mother of two children, a grandmother of one, and, at fifty-eight, I am jealous of young people today, jealous of their freedom, their frankness and the way they live and love without feeling guilty. Why was I born so early? Or so late?

I CONFESS

Answer: Your confession deserves some kind of absolution, and the best I can do is to remind you of the time when you were in your teens. My calculator tells me that that would have been in the early 1930s. To be sure, those were depression years, but, according to the record, it was also the time of the flappers, the first hint that young people were smoking, the end of the prohibition, the coming of the "sinful" drive-in theaters and the scandalous advent of the "rumble seat."

Now it may be that you didn't have anything to do with these revolutionary break-throughs, didn't indulge in either rouge or booze or spend your nights in lover's lane snuggled under a blanket in a tin lizzie; but I have a hunch that at the time, some other mother of two and grandmother of one looked at you and said to herself, "Why was *I* born so early?"

There is also a good chance that a few decades from now, your children or your grandchild will look with longing eyes at the new breed of American youth and ask with a sigh, "Why were we born so early—or so late?"

It is not a matter of time that dictates our secret life styles, it is a point of view and a sense of established values which are continually being quietly outlived or reconfirmed. Our time, your time, is *all time.* Let's have a will to believe in life unchained by calendar years, and let's be grateful for the privilege of living wisely, richly and fully, no matter what our paradoxical feelings of remorse about the fact that some of yesterday's vices have become today's virtues. You are absolved.

MB

Question: Do you think it necessary or advisable to confess one's "sins" to another person? I heard a psychologist say that in order to mend our way of living: "We must tell another person, preferably a significant other one, our every sin of thought or act. Each sin that has been committed must be recited in every detail and honestly specified. Also, we must accept, completely and unequivocably, forgiveness by another and by ourself."

I do not agree. It is my feeling that it is never necessary or advisable to confess one's "sins" to another person. Even the thought of lying on a couch and confessing to an impersonal psychiatrist is a notion I cannot abide. Our convictions are always bolstered when someone agrees with us, especially when we lack the academic training to make an educated evaluation. A person should start where he is and assume responsibility. There is no need confessing.

P. R. G.

Answer: Your subject is particularly of current interest because a Catholic priest said recently that "the confessional is up for grabs!"

I am often accused of taking a medial position in discussions about confession, but, to me, compromise of opinion is a virtue. Gandhi once said, "I value truth so much I am usually willing to compromise my convictions with those who also feel they have found truth." So, in the case of the question at hand, I feel that sometimes it is not only good but imperative that people confess their sins, and sometimes it is just as wise not to confess them.

Surely, if one has knowingly done wrong against another, amends should be made in order to live amiably with oneself, to maintain personal self-respect, no less than respect for the one "sinned" against. On the other hand, there are "sins" or personal shortcomings which do not involve others. The sublimation or resolution of such injustices can surely be worked out privately by any wise and thoughtful individual who is honest and alert to self-improvement. Judging from your letter, you are such a person because you confided to me:

"I have done several things during my life which I prefer to call mistakes in my trial-and-error search for meaning. At those moments I felt I was doing the very best my current understanding permitted. If this is rationalizing, so be it. I could not confess to another human being. I thrashed these things out in prayer and meditation and this was between God and me."

MB

Question: I have read several of your books and articles. In your travels and research, who is the most interesting person you have ever met and why was he or she so interesting?

R. S.

Answer: I am really serious when I tell you that the most interesting person I have ever met is me.

Why? Because when I think of the range of my potential, much of which I fail to use or develop, the untold blessings, most of which I fail to realize, the marvelous way I have been guided and blessed and how often I have neglected to be grateful, there is no one more interesting or complex.

I have the capacity to dream the most wonderful and outlandish dreams, to see myself in situations to which I often aspire in reality. I feel the sweep of deep emotions; I have experienced tragedy and triumph, sorrow and joy, failure and success, sin and salvation. I think I know what both Dr. Jekyll and Mr. Hyde were up to, and what all the good and bad, big and little people whom I have met have gone through at some point in their lives. I am part of them and one with them.

I do not always make the most of it, but every day in my life is a new and challenging experience, and over and above and through it all is the movement of a life and mind and power greater than my own.

No doubt about it, I am the most interesting person I have ever met, mainly, of course, because I am the only one I really presume to know. And I am sure that when you stop to think about it, you will say to *yourself,* "Of all the people I have ever met, the most interesting of all is *me.*"

MB

2

Of Creativity and Inspiration

~~~~~~

Question: How is inspiration inspired? This may be a poor way of putting it, but you know what I mean. Is it something we must wait for or pray for or work for, or does it come only to those God wants to have it?

J. J.

Answer: The literal meaning of the word *inspiration* is "the art of breathing in." With this in mind, you are ready to try an experiment. Sit quietly, erect, head up, spine straight, eyes closed, body vibrant but relaxed. Slowly breathe in and out, permitting the mind, no less than the lungs, to receive an *inspiration.* Do this seriously, joyfully, expectantly, and see what creative thoughts are channeled to you and through you.

"Inspiration is inspired," to use your phrase, by finding *life* inspiring. The more you attune yourself to life, the more rested, integrated and healthy you are, the clearer the channel for inspiration.

This is not to say that people who are not well cannot be inspired. Nor can we say that forms of inspiration and creativity do not often emerge out of smoke-filled conference rooms, rap sessions, verbal encounters, even out of marital squabbles and the like. But inspiration in the sense of highly spiritualized thought that changes, enriches and uplifts life is a breathing in and a breathing out in harmony with the presence of God. Try it.

MB

Question: Do you work by inspiration or must you think things through?

S. L.

Answer: My work—primarily research, lecturing and writing—is my inspiration. This does not rule out the need for thinking things through. To me, inspiration is the suggestion of an idea in the rough, or the hint of something to be achieved through work. My most inspiring thoughts come naturally.

MB

Question: I was asked the question, "What is God?" in one of my classes at the Unity Center in New York City. I searched in books, articles, etc., for the answers, and finally one day in total exasperation and in the middle of New York's busiest rush time I said: "God, I can't find the answer to this question. You are going to have to tell me." As clear as a bell came the answer: "I AM you becoming Me." I wrote a short poem about it:

> I turned within, in hope to see,
> And asked my God, "What can you be?"
> The answer came so clear, so free:
> "I am you becoming Me."
> I questioned on, the answers came:
> "We two are one, we are the same,
> When hands are clean, when hearts are free,
> I am you becoming Me."
> So listen well, my words to hear,
> (The still small voice, the inner ear);
> "I'll guide your way, the Truth you'll see.
> I am you now being Me."

A. L.

Answer: Thank you for sharing your thoughts. Your inspiration suggests an interesting point. The very fact of need, of sheer earnest desire, often sparks the moment of inspiration. That is why we should never give up or despair. The inspiration we earnestly seek is usually close at hand, only a thought, or, better, a breath away.

Let's try to realize that inspiration comes from *within.* "Truth work" implies this kind of a discovery. God may be "out there" somewhere but He is also the living breath, the I AM in us. One of metaphysical religion's great contributions is to demonstrate that *the awakening of self-awareness* is *the discovery of God-awareness.* The recognition of what *I* AM is a break-through in tapping an inspirational source of unlimited creativity. Your poem confirms it.

MB

Question: I know what ESP stands for, but what is it? I know it has to do with mental telepathy and extrasensory perception and that it means special mystical talents, but what is it all about?

D. K.

Answer: ESP has many connotations. In current usage, it refers to many phenomena beyond the range of sense perception. These include such powers as clairaudience, clairvoyance, mind-to-mind communication, the ability, in fact, to foresee, foretell or forecast anything from communication in outer space to dialogues with the dead.

One important ESP category toward which scholars in the field are beginning to direct their investigation is the paranormal aptitude associated with changed states of consciousness. This may be what you refer to as "special mystical talents." Mysticism, however, is more closely related to *spiritual* advancement than is ESP. Mysticism is the belief that knowledge of God is possible through a heightened state of intuitive awareness. ESP, on the other hand, as the acronym suggests, is an extra*sensory* perception. Though it is difficult to draw hard and fast lines between speculative fields, it may be inferred that mysticism is primarily related to spiritual unfoldment while ESP is concerned with the processes of parapsychological phenomena. For more information on this topic, let me suggest you read the excellent study by Karlis Osis and Edwin Eckert in the January, 1971 (vol. 65) issue of the *Journal of the American Society for Psychical Research* entitled "ESP and Changed States of Consciousness Induced by Meditation."

MB

Question: Not a question, but a thought.
I regret: to think of the years I spent *not* searching for Truth.
I rejoice: to think of the years I *will* be searching for Truth.

SAM and HARRIET

Answer: Not an answer, but a comment. When I didn't seek, I didn't know, but when I started seeking, I came to know that the knowing is in the seeking.

MB

Question: At the conclusion of *Lessons in Truth* we are told "God loves us." But during residency in a nursing home I walk down a corridor lined with patients tied to their chairs. They have as much resemblance to humans as vegetables do. Can we say in truth these humans are loved at all?

In all truth can we believe God's love has been with victims of Vietnam and Hiroshima, to name only two of the many? Do I have a sane right to believe in healing, that through faith, God will normalize my gums so that my dentures will hold? This is to name but one of the numerous changes that has come to my eighty-three-year-old body.

M. T. N.

Answer: Questions such as you raised in your letter have been asked since the dawn of humankind's face-to-face relationship with God. A loving God—suffering humankind: these two seemingly irreconcilable entities are the central figures in all the world's scriptures and in much of the world's great literature, music and art. They have given rise to all sorts of theological arguments, rationalizations and philosophical speculations. Is suffering an illusion, the result of carnal belief, estrangement from good or disobedience to divine law? Because human beings are free, do they bring suffering upon themselves? In the Judeo-Christian tradition, the theme of human suffering runs from Job to Jesus and is majestically treated from Genesis to Revelation. Many explanations are hinted at, but always there is the nursing home corridor, as you say, and there is Hiroshima and, fully as inexplicable, there are natural tragedies.

Before the time of Christ, the philosopher Epicurus, in thinking about the problem of unexplained and seemingly undeserved suffering, dashed off a challenge to both God and humanity. He said: "Is God willing to prevent evil and not able? Then He is impotent. Is He able but not willing? Then He is malevolent. Is He both able and willing? Then whence comes evil and suffering? Is He neither able nor willing? Then why call Him divine?"

With the coming of Jesus a new light of inspiration lit up the world. Among other creative truths introduced by the Galilean was the profound concept of a loving Father who, being love, was also law and life. Herein lies both the answer to the problem of suffering and the continuing quest: a personally knowable but never fully comprehensible God, realizable through faith, which became the very heart of religion and the secret of our oneness with Him. It was this message that generated *our* love and challenged us to demonstrate it in our individual lives.

The nursing home corridor, Hiroshima, natural tragedies say to us, "Come, show *your* love!" Here is the miracle: it is only as we love more that God uses us as a channel for more of His love and only through our love is His love more fully understood.

MB

Question: The other night I caught you on Unity's *Word* program on TV. It sent me to the dictionary to look up the word you talked about: *serendipity.* Webster gives the meaning of the word, but my question is: were there really three princes of Serendip, or is the whole Walpole story a put-on?

JERRY C.

Answer: It's serendipitous that you should ask. The question comes up every once in a while and the dictionary definition is all too brief.

Horace Walpole, eighteenth century litterateur, coined the word *serendipity* after reading the fable *The Three Princes of Serendip.* You can read it too if you have access to a good-sized library. Ask for the *Peregrinaggio* by Heinrich Gassner (International Scholarly Book Service, 1970, Forest Grove, Oregon). Though it is not known whether there actually were three princes, it has been established that Serendip (or Serendib) was the ancient name of Ceylon. And it is conceivable that there actually were three hip sons of a king who left home to wander through the world, as the story says.

Webster's International Dictionary gives the meaning of *serendipity* as "the gift of finding valuable or agreeable things not sought for." Left untold is the deeper meaning which recent interpreters have suggested for the word, namely, that the discovery may not be chance but, rather, the working of a causal law. Fate may not be fate; it could be the *effect* of a hidden *cause,* and destiny may actually *be* the working of a karmic law. At any rate, serendipity and the three princes suggest that whatever happens to us justifies a deeper look, and that often what we think is driving us off course may actually be putting us back on the *right* course.

Why did what happened happen? Serendipity says it happened either for our growth or for our guidance; it happened either by conscious or unconscious forces within ourselves; it happened, if not for our benefit, then for the benefit and profit of someone else. Such reasoning, you must admit, covers practically all of the options and is a typically serendipitous discovery.

MB

3

Of Techniques to Live By

~~~~~~

Question: What do you think about taking up collections at church services? Isn't it a somewhat wordly practice, smacking of commercialism? Wouldn't it be better just to have baskets at the door, or not take up offerings at all, trusting in God to "offer and increase"?

KATHY

Answer: Your name makes me think you are young, but the views you express are as old as the hills. Pastors and lay people have raised questions about Sunday fund-raising for years. Many ministers feel it would be more appropriate aesthetically *not* to pass the plate and, as you say, simply trust the Lord for the increase. The inference is that these ministers apparently trust the Lord but do not trust the people. The people need a bit of nudging and the sacramental offertory, plates and all, has therefore become part of the ritual. Tithing, or giving in any form, can be an important technique for daily living. It is the giver *and* the spirit of giving that are important.

The method of giving in metaphysical churches, a method now practiced in traditional churches as well, has always impressed me. This part of the service is looked upon not as a put-on but as a privilege, not as a commercial act but as an act of worship. The technique is to clasp the offering thoughtfully between the palms of the hands, close the eyes and be grateful for God's blessing and bounty, recognizing that in the offering you are merely returning to the creative Source that which the Source has entrusted to you. Clasping your offering warmly, believe and know that "Divine love blesses, increases and multiplies all that we give and all that we receive." Place your offering in the plate or basket and think, not of money, but of the partnership between God and you, giving in love, loving to give, making the offering a beautiful and indispensable part of worship.

MB

Question: One year ago, feeling that something was missing in my life, I embarked upon a sincere and faithful Christian endeavor program. At that time I was earning eight hundred dollars monthly as an advertising agency artist and launching a fine art career. The attached year-end record sheet can best describe my problem. What went wrong?

1. I tithe 10 percent or more faithfully.
2. I trust God to direct my affairs and make them prosper.
3. I pray and meditate each day, affirming good for my career.
4. To the very best of my ability, I express love, compassion and tolerance toward everyone.
5. I repeatedly pray for the healing of a minor affliction.
6. Daily I ask Christ to come into my heart.

1. I am deplorably deep in debt and in need of welfare.
2. Several months ago my agency earnings came to an end. I now earn thirty dollars per week.
3. My paintings are not selling, although I've been accepted by the leading galleries.
4. All my former friends ignore me, and I have not one new friend.
5. My health is poor and my energy is fast depleting.
6. I am chronically depressed and losing hope.

D. E. A.

Answer: The audit of your adventure in faith is interesting—and provocative. What was your goal—money, success and recognition, or learning more about God's way and God's will? From a mystical point of view, your desire to achieve what you wanted was more intense than your wish to learn His way.

Your letter deserves more consideration than this because it resembles the sort of balance sheet many of us have drawn up at some time during the quest in the hope that the Lord would reconsider our plight.

It is at this point that we make our first mistake, for we are thinking in terms of God as humanly conceived—instead of God as divinely known and understood. If the working and guidance of God is to be trusted but does not work as we want it to, then either our understanding of God or our own integrity in the matter is at fault. To put it bluntly, God is always right, though He may seem to us to be wrong. Such is His nature by definition and decree, and such is the basis of true belief in Divine Principle. Lacking full acceptance of this "truth," we have a compulsive desire to blame Him and excuse ourselves.

Second, let's ask ourselves whether we are thinking too much in terms of external rewards, and not enough in terms of inner spiritual growth. Let's reassess our sense of values. Do we tithe money only to get it back in return? "There are many kinds of banks," as a friend of mine says. True, love doesn't pay the rent, and compliments do not make the payments on the car. But, interestingly, when we accept our *spiritual* good as the channel for *material* good, there comes a time when no line can be drawn between the one and the other.

Third, God will not be put on the bargaining block. He does not respond to challenge. He responds to cooperation. Often prayer and meditation, wrongly directed toward making demands on Him, even thwart the prompting of our reason. We make God objective, anthropomorphic, "out there" somewhere, instead of inwardly present and expressive in our lives.

Write another letter to God. Draw up another balance sheet. Dig deeper into your consciousness and make another audit if you want to play the game this way. Tell Him what you have to be grateful for.

Let's also take another look at your complaint that you have lost all of your former friends. Strictly speaking, there is no such thing as losing a true friend. True friends cannot be lost. If they leave you or ignore you, they weren't really true friends in the first place. Instead of praying daily for Christ to come into your heart (forgive the preaching), take time to hear Him say, "I am already here."

Your letter reflects so much of the doubt and complaining lurking in those whose "minor" afflictions become major, overwhelming problems. And, as always, what is actually happening is this: Divine Mind is trying to get a message through to us—through to you! The very fact that you wrote as you did indicates that God is truly interested in your adventure in faith. Who knows, your present problems may be a stage of your unfolding "Christian endeavor program." Write again sometime and tell us what has gone right!

MB

Question: Several of my friends who feel close to Pentecostal teachings have tried to arouse my enthusiasm. However, I feel true mysticism is quite different (from the Pentecostal experience), yet I lack words to express this difference. How do we correlate the rebirth experience of the well-known mystics with the rebirths of the Pentecostals and their experiences of the Baptism by the Spirit and speaking in tongues?

E. F. G.

Answer: The only valid correlation is in the area of awareness and insight. In both Christian mystical experience and the Pentecostal encounter, Christ-centeredness is the fire and passion of a "new birth" or "rebirth." Here the similarity ends.

The mystic becomes deeply reflective, inward looking, soul-searching, contemplative. The Pentecostal becomes evangelistic, spiritually extroverted, eager for conquest and dedicated to the Great Commission: "Go ye therefore, and teach all nations, baptizing them in the name of the Father, and of the Son, and of the Holy Ghost" (Matt. 28:19 KJV).

The true Christian mystic is a sensitive, the true Pentecostal is a zealot. The first draws God's world around him, the second seeks to draw others into what he believes to be God's true world.

The mystic considers it his duty to plant and nourish spiritual values. The Pentecostal believes it is his mission to harvest them.

And so it is.

MB

Question: Why and how should a person tithe?

J. B.

Answer: Why? Because of gratitude. How? Generously.

MB

Question: I was taught that I am a rich child of a rich Father, that I am a child of God and heir to His kingdom. I am a daily active seeker of Truth, and desire to become all God fashioned me to be. In my search for God and Truth, I desire to pray, meditate, contemplate, say affirmations and denials, tithe my earnings and serve whatever way I can at the Unity center here. In short, Unity and its teachings have become a way of life for me, and I thank God every day that we found each other.

My questions are:

1. When two people of opposites are married and make togetherness a reality, does good come to one as to the other? Can I, for example, seek prosperity and receive it without it happening to my husband? I want nothing but the best for him, but I am kind of hung up on seekers and nonseekers sharing and sharing alike. Does it happen this way? It's a minor question, but it bugs me.

2. About loneliness. My friends don't fit the same places they used to in my life, my own desires and needs being different. Some quite frankly think I'm nuts because I work at spiritual understanding. I know I am never alone, for wherever I am, God is. But it seems I have a longing, a lonesomeness I am not really able to define. I feel a deep, abiding need for someone to share something with me. I don't really know how to say it. Can you please help me on my two questions?

R. C.

Answer: The rich ring of your letter tells me that all is well. That much is obvious. Because of this awareness, I feel your questions will benefit all our readers.

1. Togetherness as a working reality also implies separateness. Marriage may make two persons one, but it may also inspire greater individualization. In this connection, the enrichment caused by opposites is obvious. Wouldn't it be monotonous if a couple were homogenous?

In his essay on "Marriage" Kahlil Gibran suggests that the ceremony does not imply possession of one person by the other, but a complementing and completing of each other. Prosperity can "happen" to you without it happening to your husband, but when it happens to you, remember that he too may gain because of your complementary relationship.

There is in astronomy a phenomenon called the binary system in which two stars revolve around each other under the influence of mutual gravitational attraction. To the naked eye, the stars appear to be one, but through a telescope they are seen to be separate entities revolving around a common center. Think about your relationship with your husband along these lines and you may find an answer to your question.

2. Loneliness. Some friends are not forever. In a changing world, in the inevitable transmutation of our thoughts and characters, particularly in the midst of the quest for spiritual insight and spiritual understanding, we must often let go of others, and they must let go of us. True friends understand this and such understanding is the very basis of friendship.

Though you will find new friends continually tuning into the wave length of your need, keep a segment of your heart for the divine loneliness and be careful not to fill it for the sake of assuaging the pain of growth. The most profound manifestation of love is love that transcends loneliness, rather than love that is meant simply to remove it. This is the love that the life of Jesus exemplifies. People share themselves with Him and He with them because of His rare insight into this universal longing of the human heart.

MB

Question: My questions are:

1. What or who is the Devil? My personal background does not include the Devil. He (it) seems like an easy cop-out. How does a wrong choice become possible if God has created only good?

2. Can the Devil heal? I was at a recent healing service featuring Emilie Gardner Neal, who said the Devil could heal physical ills. Surely, healing of body, mind or spirit should come only from God.

NO NAME

Answer: It is difficult to describe someone you don't really know. However, though your personal background does not include the Devil, mine does. I heard about him from my preacher uncle and my preacher brother and my preacher cousins. They insisted he was as real as sin and as big as life. That was why I had to let him go. They made him too big. Bigger than God. I had to get him off my back.

He was too mean, too conniving, too presumptuous in his attempt to challenge the omnipotent, omniscient and omnipresent Creator. I was helped in my encounter with the Devil by the metaphysical view that he is "the deceiving phase of mind in man that has fixed ideas in opposition to Truth."

As to your question about the wrong choice, it seems to me that the more a person grows in spiritual understanding, the more he realizes that wrong is often a hidden right. A wrong choice is right in the lessons of growth we learn from it. A wrong thought is right in strengthening us by our overcoming of it. A wrong deed is right when it teaches us the immutability of God's law. A wrong friend is right in helping us discover the meaning of true friendship. A wrong note, as Brahms once said, may be a stepping-stone to the right one. Look at it this way: a wrong choice is possible because God *has* created only good.

Can the Devil heal? Health or integrative oneness, like heaven is, as Charles Fillmore, founder of the Unity movement, pointed out, "conscious harmony. When this harmony is invaded by a thought adverse to divine law, there is Satan in the midst of things and there is war in heaven. When the Christ declares the Truth, error-thought falls away, which is to say that *Satan* falls away as speedily as lightning from heaven." If this is what Neal meant by the Devil's capacity to heal physical ills, it poses an interesting problem, because without the recognition and rejection of him (it) as a "deceiving thought," healing might not take place.

To sum up what I have been saying, evil may often be good in the making, and the devil (let's use a small "d" just for the devil of it) may well lead a person to a higher concept of God.

MB

Question: What is meant by "picturization"?

CYNTHIA K.

Answer: Picturization, treasure-maping, visualization, thought-ography are metaphysical terms suggesting a technique in which *imagination, affirmation* and *emanation* play a triple role in effecting a desired *realization.*

Here is how it works. Picture yourself well and strong, or prosperous and successful, or whatever it is you want or sincerely feel you need. Hold the image ineffably in mind. Affirm deep within yourself that the imaged goal is being reached and finally that the thing you picturize has come to pass. Surround or infuse your goal with the vital force (innate life-force) continually emanating from the spirit within you, and become what you have picturized. This is the general principle of picturization. It can, of course, be applied to objective no less than to subjective situations or needs. Mind is the master. God is the guide.

MB

Question: I read with relief your answer to a question in which you stressed the need for a deeper discovery of the "God-in-me" before getting enmeshed in seminars and workshop programs. Perhaps if I stood on really firm ground I would not need reassurance, but the urging in publications to do more, be more, can be unsettling.

Finding the balance between being something to others and being something to yourself presupposes you have already found your center of gravity within yourself. The majority of people I come in contact with have not found this balance. Finding the fine line of relatedness to others without becoming submerged requires an impartial objectivity which I, as a woman long involved with raising a family, have not acquired.

People in my generation are physically tired, yet continue to work hard in a one-sided commitment that leaves the spiritual side of their growth undeveloped. I feel a desire to develop inwardly, yet the urgings to conform to what is expected of me are still strong.

P. L.

Answer: Your letter carried the resounding echo of so much correspondence that comes to me that I wish I could have quoted it in full. The challenges of our times and the deep-seated feeling that we are not doing enough or cannot do more often conjure up a sense of guilt similar to that formerly evoked by opinions that we were conceived and born in sin.

Let's learn from the past. Let's take a fresh look at our capabilities. Let's do our best and leave the rest to God.

I say this because the fallout of the past is still upon us. During the

Vietnam tragedy we were reminded by evangelists, psychologists and politicians that we all were guilty. And Watergate, we were assured, was everyone's fault. Now we are warned that we have all helped perpetrate the rise in crime and are *all* to blame for the misdeeds of our children.

Metaphysical movements have no intention of making you or me caretaker or custodian of the world. Their aim is to develop a sense of spiritual awareness, a rise in consciousness, which can guide us through life.

The center of gravity, that's the point. Begin at your center of gravity. You are *right* where you are. Do your service to others without losing your balance. As you feel your balance improve, quietly improve your service. It is all reciprocal. A good teacher will ask you to do your best but will not frustrate you by demanding the impossible.

MB

4

Of Love and Marriage

~~~~~~~~~~~~~~~~~~~~~~~~~~~~~~~~~

Question: I feel guilty when I love. Can you understand that, and if so, what's the matter with me?

<div align="right">SERIOUSLY</div>

Answer: It is quite simple. You love to feel guilty.

<div align="right">MB</div>

Question: During the last few years of my husband's life he was an invalid, completely dependent on me. I did everything I could for him even though our marriage had not been a very happy one. Down deep, though, I resented having to do things for him for so long. Now that he is gone, I can't forgive myself for having felt resentful. How can I rid myself of these terrible feelings of guilt?

<div align="right">P. R.</div>

Answer: You are surely not alone in your feelings of guilt. There are countless people who could, if conscientious, write a letter similar to yours.

It has long been a pet theory of mine that the greater our capacity for love and service, the greater our tendency to feel that we should and could have done more for someone. But the more we condemn ourselves for being inadequate, the deeper our frustration. We *are* human and divine. There *are* times when the spirit is willing and the flesh is weak, as well as the other way around.

We should learn to forgive ourselves for our "humanness." We all grow weary of doing good at times. We all wonder at times about our lot, our seeming inability to do our best and fulfill our appointed missions in life. In fact, even top-of-the-world people often wonder whether they have really found their lifework or fulfilled their assignments. All of which is not intended to assuage our sense of inadequacy, but to point out that if the gap between our ideals and our performances is so universal, we should not live in the past and nurse our frustrations. "Religion," as William James once said, "should make easy and felicitous that which in any case is necessary."

It is a major function of religion to remind us that every day, every hour, every moment provides a chance for a fresh start in life. This may be one of religion's most practical principles and greatest distinctions. Furthermore, guilt is so closely allied with self-pity and is so often an excuse for escape that the sooner we face the new day with hope and a sense of release, the sooner we find our way into a new life. The freer love is from guilt, the greater love's power. In my years of research I have found no more insightful approach than to "do your best and leave the rest to God." That's why He's there—or, better, *here.*

MB

Question: I have been praying for more than twenty years for just one thing: for my husband to return to me, or to find a companion. We had five children, all of whom are married and have children of their own. I am very lonely. I was in my late thirties. Now I am in my fifties. Do you think my prayer will ever be answered?

M. C.

Answer: If in twenty long years it never occurred to you to release your husband (and yourself) from this burden of possessiveness, let me suggest it now. In the first place, it is no virtue to "pray without ceasing" unless you use your God-given intelligence to help in working out an answer to prayer. Second, prayer that leaves no room for God's will is not a prayer but a command. It merely increases loneliness and itself becomes a burden. *Let go!*

Chances are that your prayer was answered long, long ago, though not the way you wanted it to be. The time has come for you to close the book on this game and quietly say: "Thank You, Father. Your wisdom is greater than mine."

Find new interests, new areas of activity; get yourself off your hands, and don't order God around, but trust in His fellowship, guidance and love. Let life begin at fifty! It can if you will, and it will if you can.

MB

Question: My husband and I are very much in love and after six years of married life feel that we are one of the happiest couples in the world, with two lovely children, a boy and a girl. We often ask ourselves, why, then, when we have a quarrel, as we sometimes do, is it such a big quarrel, a real blow, over some little thing? At such times we wonder, do we really love each other as much as we think? If people are in love, why should they ever quarrel?

L. T.

Answer: The more perfect a symphony, the more annoyed are the players at their lack of perfection. The greater the artist, the more critical he is of his art. The deeper the love, perhaps the more critical and impatient the lovers, knowing they have the capacity for "perfection."

Nature, being related to divinity, sheds light on your question. Consider the cleansing effect of a thundershower, or the beauty of the calm after a storm, or even the sense of quiet after an earth tremor. Perfect love, like perfect peace, is an idyllic concept, a utopian thought to sing about and to strive for; but if we actually reached perfection, it would be monotonously dull and dry—to live without occasional rain and a bit of a blow at times.

Kiss and make up.

MB

Question: My husband and I have a question and a concern. In the Midwestern town where we live, it is embarrassing to have a son who lives with a girl without being married. We love both of them and they love us, but they think we are old-fashioned to think they should be married. We are embarrassed when they come to visit and share the same room, just as if they were married. Fortunately there are no children, but this could happen. Do you think we are old-fashioned?

CONCERNED PARENTS

Answer: Yes. But what's wrong with being old-fashioned? Your son and his girl friend are "new-fashioned," and they see nothing wrong with *that.* Both of you are couples caught in the web of change. Make the best of it.

How to do it? In the light—or dark—of a radically, rapidly changing world, the best we can do is manifest God's love and reveal God's will as it appears to us. Judging from your report, this is what you are doing, and if this is what your son and his girl friend are doing, the confrontation is not with the town, but with your respective convictions of morality and truth.

You are involved in a social change and not apart *from* it. It is your adventure and challenge. And theirs. Discuss the situation with them once more in the light of spiritual growth and spiritual understanding. Let me know what happens.

MB

Question: Would you kindly elaborate on Eph. 5:22–23. Does it mean exactly what it says?

J. F.

Answer: Here is the text you refer to: "Wives, be subject to your husbands, as to the Lord. For the husband is the head of the wife as Christ is the head of the church, His body, and is Himself its Savior."

Was it meant literally? Does it mean what it says? Yes. Paul (or whoever wrote the letter) was addressing a dissident religious community. There was discord in both the family and in the church. The writer was equally interested in saving both, and his cross-references between the two are dramatic and clear if you read the entire letter.

Though the writer requires much of wives, he is equally demanding of husbands: "Husbands, love your wives, as Christ loved the church and gave Himself up for her. . . . Even so husbands should love their wives as their own bodies."

MB

Question: I would like to relate my experience with marriage and premarital relations. God's law is love. What then is man's law?

I have a grown daughter, and two grown sons who are twins. My daughter and one of my sons are now divorced. My other son married and stayed married. He has two children, a boy and a girl. They live only six miles from here, but I never get to see them because his wife likes to bug me too much.

My son who was divorced is living with a girl named Joanne. They have been living together for three years. She is gentle and kind and does nice things for us. Joanne calls me Mom and shows me respect. Dian, who is my legal daughter-in-law, won't show respect for anyone. Not even in front of her own children.

What is an open vow? Joanne said she and Tom made open vows to each other. Please answer that question. If not for me, then answer it for the public, the ones who are worried about these laws. I am not afraid anymore since I met gentle Joanne.

Mrs. A. C.

Answer: Man's law should entail obedience to and a reflection of God's law. Ideally, our *love* should also be a reflection of God's love. From this point of view, you should love Dian even though she bugs you. Perhaps your continual comparison of Dian and Joanne has gotten in the way of a solution to the problem. Have you tried loving her, and through meditation and affirmation tried to change the vibrations that exist between her and you? There is always something about anyone that is worthy of love!

As to open vows: among the young people of the "frank generation" the term refers to pacts or agreements made on faith and profession of love, rather than on legal or statutory arrangements. Rebellion against peers, against the "establishment" and the institutionalized church led to an increase in civil, as opposed to ecclesiastical marriages.

Evidently, some young people want to prove that they can live together as man and wife by virtue of their own promises, as is being demonstrated, apparently, by Tom and Joanne.

MB

Question: Who is right? My husband says he can have an affair with another woman without having it lessen his love for me. I say this is impossible. If no one can serve two masters, no one can serve two loves. What do you say?

TROUBLED

Answer: Is this a hypothetical case or *is* he having an affair with another woman? Is this something you simply talk about and speculate about or *is* it for him a fait accompli? If the latter, you will be able to tell whether or not his love for you has changed. Sexual faithfulness is surely one of the commitments of true love, and infidelity (no matter how archaic the *word*) is a tricky and complicated way to increase fidelity, no matter what the experts say or how the husband rationalizes his behavior.

MB

5

Of Health and Fitness

~~~~~~.

Question: I once heard you mention ten things that long-living people around the world have in common. Would appreciate it if you repeated these practices in *Questions on the Quest.*

R. B.

Answer:

1. They all remain active, walk more than they ride, and they all work.

2. They all have a low caloric intake. The average daily intake for long-living people is between fifteen hundred and seventeen hundred. For the average American, by contrast, the count is between twenty-four hundred and twenty-six hundred per day.

3. They eat slowly. They chew their food. They maintain a happy, healthy attitude when eating.

4. They affirm long life. None of this "three-score years and ten." They are mentally geared to becoming centenarians, at least.

5. Their attitude toward life is wholesome, open-minded and oriented toward joy of living.

6. They have pure air to breathe, pure water to drink and organic gardens to provide their food.

7. They are not hung up on thoughts of retirement, social security, welfare, generation gaps, senior citizenry and the inevitability of aging.

8. They deviate little from their established way of life. They rarely move or change their habits or style of life.

9. They have a hopeful philosophy of life, admiration for slender waistlines and an appreciation of the wisdom that comes with maturity.

10. They have been wise in choosing their ancestors!

MB

Question: Have you ever been at Lourdes? Do you believe that miracles happen there?

?

Answer: Several visits to Lourdes and an interest in the "miracle cures" at France's famous healing grotto constituted a major project of mine some twelve years ago. I have not been back since. It seems to me that the popularity of this famous town at the foot of the Pyrenees peaked with "The Song of Bernadette," and with a growing awareness that the greatest shrine of healing is not a locale but a state of consciousness found within each individual. However, obviously "miracles" still occur at Lourdes. They occur wherever the shrine of consciousness is intensified.

MB

Question: Is it proper to refer to Harry Edwards, the great English spiritual healer, as a "psychic healer"? This sounds misleading to me.

D. M.

Answer: Some years ago, when I interviewed Mr. Edwards in Burrows Lea, Shere, Surrey, we talked about the various forms of healing. As I recall, he considered "spiritual healing" a general term applicable to all healing in which spiritual power predominates.

He referred to his own technique in this field as an attunement to unseen spirit healers or spirit guides. He considered himself an instrument or channel used by these entities. His approach is, therefore, neither strictly spiritual healing in the sense of the laying on of hands, nor is it magnetic healing, though it may have some similarity to both.

Strictly speaking, Edwards works in the field of *psychism,* that is, in harmony with "doctors" in the spirit world. Since disease is frequently the result of dissonance or nonattunement between the spiritual body and the physical body of the patient, a spirit guide or a "doctor in spirit" can discern, study and treat the spirit body because he himself is spirit. In this way, the "spirit doctor" guides and directs the healer, in this instance, Edwards, to the proper mode of treatment. Sometimes spirit healing involves the laying on of hands at the points where channeling is needed, but it can also take the form of "absent treatment," or treatment at a distance, where no tactile contact is made. In any case, "psychic healer," as a way of referring to Mr. Edwards, is okay.

MB

Question: You once published an affirmation pertaining to eyes. Would you restate it?

ELLA W.

Answer: "The light of life is the Eye, and God is that light!"
MB

Question: Do you think it is wrong or sinful to smoke?

L. T.

Answer: Smoking is an affair of the individual conscience insofar as its relationship to morals is concerned, and it is an affair of consciousness as to its spiritual implications. In moral terms, it belongs in the field of the adiaphorous, that is, something neither right nor wrong, neither beneficial nor harmful, unless it causes offense or inconvenience to others.

In spiritual terms, smoking depends on your interpretation of what, for you, constitutes spirituality, anything from aesthetics to your philosophical interpretation of Scripture. There is no text in the Good Book which says, "Thou shalt not smoke," but there *are* implicit references to respecting the body as the "temple of God."

As for the health factor, modern research has proved beyond the shadow of doubt that smoking is physically injurious. More than that, it not only pollutes the "temple of God," it smells up the house and pollutes others.

There is a good possibility that your continuing quest for spiritual growth will provide the answer you need. Chances are, you won't have to give up smoking. It will give you up.

MB

Question: Where does Unity stand on vegetarianism, and what does it have to say about eating habits generally?

JACK

Answer: Unity teachings are broad and inclusive. In my book, *The Unity Way of Life,* I said that "Unity has shallows in which a child can wade, and depths in which a giant must swim." Its teaching in regard to eating habits in general and to vegetarianism in particular are more implicit than explicit. Charles Fillmore was a vegetarian. The earliest cafeteria at Unity Headquarters didn't serve meat. The overall teaching, however, can best be summed up in the Unity belief that the body *is* the temple of God and that each individual should respect it as such. As you progress in spiritual growth your consciousness grows, and as your consciousness increases you grow spiritually.

Unity would agree in principle with nutritionist Elsie Sokol of Toronto's Branson Hospital, who announced that "a balanced diet is the key to health, but people ignore this fact until a breakdown occurs." Individuals, she said, must take personal responsibility for their health.

MB

Question: I recently lost my near vision. Medical science cannot help me and now my only hope seems to be the Source of all good, God. I have been a metaphysical student for thirty years. I have used every form of prayer and meditation I know, but my eyes are no better. I would appreciate any suggestions you may have to give.

MRS. G. L.

Answer: Our Source of all good is *always* God, whether medical science can help us or not. God works through many channels, from science to seemingly chance happenings. Don't give up.

It would, of course, be unwise for me to give advice merely on the strength of your letter. However, since your question reached me while I am reading a book on nutrition, I take this as a sign to make a suggestion because the book contains an interesting reference to an eye condition (seemingly something like yours) which responded miraculously to a juice diet.

If you have never looked into nutritional therapy, you might want to now, while continuing your program of prayer and meditation. The book I recommend is *The Complete Handbook of Nutrition* by Gary and Steve Null (Dell Publishing Co. Inc., New York).

MB

Question: Here is my theory of spiritual healing. Please comment.

1. The subconscious mind controls body functions: breathing, circulation, digestion, body chemistry, glandular secretions, healing of wounds, etc.

2. The subconscious is also the realm of feeling: love, joy, sorrow, hate, guilt, resentment, etc.

3. Destructive emotions disturb the subconscious so that it cannot properly take care of the body functions and disease or disability results.

4. Faith calms the disturbed subconscious. The cause of body ills is removed, proper functions are restored, healing takes place. Christ explained this when He said that by faith are we healed.

I do not think Christ worked this out "one, two, three, four"; He just explained a built-in feature of the body: God's holy temple. Perhaps my outline will stimulate some thinking and help some unbelievers.

M. B.

Answer: And some believers, too. Many of our readers may want to judge for themselves the logic, value and validity of your four points. Surely, it is an insight into the search for a better understanding of the nature of health and well-being.

MB

Question: Who said, "Make food your medicine, not medicine your food"?

C. C.

Answer: Hippocrates, about 400 B.C.

MB

Question: If you suffered from headaches, as I have for five years, and no drugs or doctors or chiropractors helped, not even spiritual healers, what would you do?

A. L. T.

Answer: I'd fast and pray under the direction of someone skilled in the field of prayer and fasting.

MB

Question: I am writing to you about a problem I have. I have studied Unity books and magazines for years and they give me great understanding of myself and God and peace of mind.

But one thing I can't cope with is that when something unpleasant happens, I lose my temper. It is then that I need help badly, because when I get angry and lose my temper, everything I learned and studied just slips out of my mind, and in those moments my anger is in control over me. If I could only remember God's teachings instead of blowing up, I would be doing just fine.

I tell myself that by letting off steam I may never have high blood pressure, but I hate to hurt people's feelings. What would be your suggestion? I am a Sagittarian, born December 8. Please don't use my name.

S. S.

Answer: If you have really and truly applied Unity principles and practices in your life (instead of just reading about them!), if you have done your best mentally and spiritually to control your temper, I would suggest you check your diet. What foods are you eating? What are your eating habits?

I recently had a highly rewarding talk with Professor Ralph Bolton of Pomona College. He had just returned from near Lake Titicaca in Peru, where he had conducted a thorough study of the Qolla people, who lose their tempers faster and more furiously than any other group on record. Many reasons have been advanced to explain the behavior of the Qollas, but Professor Bolton was the first to argue that the cause lay not in their heads but in their stomachs!

He discovered that the Qollas suffered from hypoglycemia. When their blood sugar dropped, their tempers flared because the excitement pumped glucose into their blood. Thus, they felt better when they acted worse! With a new diet, however, their dispositions improved. So eat properly, apply your Unity teachings and take it easy!

MB

Question: Do you think that Jesus actually fasted for forty days, or is this a figure of speech. If He did, why did He?

W. W.

Answer: It was an established belief among people of many religions before the coming of the Christian era that sustained fasting, properly carried out, would be conducive to heightened spiritual enlightenment. The efficacy of fasting had been proved by members of the Pythagorean School, by devotees of other esoteric groups, no less than by sadhus and other holy men of India. The practice was part of the Jewish tradition, and the Pharisees fasted two days a week.

Jesus surely knew of the fasting tradition, and being what He was, He no doubt believed in it Himself. "The fast of faith" was self-confirming. He fasted to prepare Himself for His ministry and to gain clearer insight into His mission. And I have no doubt that He rigorously kept His forty foodless days more faithfully than even the best of us have ever kept the forty days of Lent.

Interesting is the fact that, as a quipster puts it, "The blessings of eating are fleeting, but the blessings of fasting are lasting!"

MB

6

Of Stress and Strain

~~~~~~~~~~~~~~~~~~~~~~~~~~~

Question: I am often filled with fear, fear of life and fear of death. I wonder what you would say to help someone like me?

<div align="right">L. A.</div>

Answer: Search your feeling of fear and see where, how and why it originated. Bring the truth of it into clear and honest perspective. Make restitution to remove its cause if restitution is needed.

Learn to affirm, "The Christ in me casts out all fear." Affirmations are a way of "speaking the word," establishing a new image in mind. The law of affirmations is: *as you affirm so you become.*

Fear is not good because it is not of God. God is love and infinite truth, fear is false and finite error.

<div align="right">MB</div>

Question: Do you believe in exorcism? Do you believe that wearing a cross will help ward off evil spirits?

<div align="right">Mrs. M. P.</div>

Answer: I believe in the rite of exorcism only in cases where the person needing help believes in it and requests it from a qualified exorcist, if such there be. My reason for taking this position is that I feel there are those so "possessed" that neither logic nor analysis, neither faith nor prayer has any effect. In such cases, the exorcist's ritual, if believed in, may prove helpful and curative.

Check this view out with your interpretation of scripture. Exorcism is mentioned only once in the Bible, Acts 19:13. However, exorcism is implied in many other passages. You may want to check Matt. 12:28, Mark 9:29, Luke 4:35 and John 15:5.

Jesus is credited with driving out malevolent spirits by His own power and authority rather than by any magical incantation or mystical formula, but exorcism predates the Christian era and is found in abundance among animistic religions. In these religions, the shaman or holy person or physician-priest drove evil spirits, not only out of people, but out of homes, valleys, groves, and other places.

Now about the power of a cross. Catholicism has always taken the rite of exorcism seriously, and this is one reason why the cross is so closely related to protective custody. The cross, however, antedates Christianity, and no one knows its precise origin. Exorcists and spiritualists believe that wearing a cross may guard against evil, but to actually "exorcise" evil entities, more is needed than wearing a cross or simply making the sign of the cross.

A spiritualist, J. J. Morse, after considerable delving into the subject of exorcism, said, "As long as evil men live on earth and die and live beyond, just so long will it be possible for their spirits to possess people."

Now, we may not agree with that, but we might give a thought to his advice for preventing such "possession." Morse said: "The greatest preventive is to cultivate your will power. Be master of yourself. Assert your right to select your own influences. Refuse to entertain unclean thoughts. Give up gross living and work toward purity of mind. By such aspiration and prayer you not only ward off but prevent the influence of undesirable spirits. This, together with a steadfast will, is the best 'exorcism' that can possibly be practiced."

But those who cannot or will not heed Morse's advice, those who lack faith and logic and who have not grasped the metaphysical truth that their life is God's life, will always find self-styled exorcists waiting for them in the wings.

MB

Question: I took my magazine copy of *Questions on the Quest* with me on a flight overseas and have been reading it up here in the friendly skies. Hence this airline stationery. I have never written to anyone for advice and cannot imagine why people cannot settle their own problems and answer their own questions. Doesn't your department simply encourage people to depend on you or someone else? Why can't people see that life is easy and simple and that we ourselves make it complicated?

G. A.

Answer: The reason people do not see life as you do is that their skies are apparently not always friendly, and they evidently do not have your particular easy-going flight pattern. Perhaps your letter will help other passengers in "the flight of life" to relax, keep their seat belts lightly fastened and enjoy the trip.

MB

Question: How can I get over my terrible sense of depression? I am sure that some of it is hereditary because when I was a child my mother started her days by telling us children how terrible she always felt. But what can I do about it? The last thirty days have been especially bad.

WORRIED

Answer: What you call hereditary may be morbid remembrance, for which metaphysicians recommend some special work in oblivescence, the art of forgetting.

You have your life to live *now,* fully, happily, intelligently. Moods, depressions, no less than many bodily maladies, cannot exist outside of a percipient mind. That is, they exist in us as thoughts, ideas and feelings that gradually dominate us if we permit them, but if we remove them from our mind, their influence will vanish, as metaphysician W. F. Evans said, "as surely as the removal of an object from before a mirror will cause the disappearance of its reflected image."

Have you had a physical examination to determine whether you need any medical or non-allopathic attention? Are you overworked, overworried or overweight? What about your major interests, enjoyments or commitments that may help get yourself off your hands? How about developing a spiritual philosophy and beginning your days on a *hopeful* note? Treat yourself to a new thirty-day test!

MB

Question: How do people solve their problems in our kind of world? Few people that I know are able to do it, no matter what their claims may be. Life in my family of three teenage children and a husband who is a department store manager is one mad rush. I work, too, to make ends meet. Weekends, when we try to get away from it all, are usually wild. So wild that my thinking is no longer clear on what to do. Most of my friends are in the same boat. Some of their boats have sunk. Ours might sink at any time. I was given several copies of *Unity* and thought I would write.

M. L. C.

Answer: Your reference to sinking boats can be a lifesaver. If you have as light a touch as your letter seems to indicate, I am convinced that as far as your boat is concerned, you can steer it into calmer seas.

The best answer to your question is, "Seek some solitude." Call it meditation, a retreat, or what you will, you need first of all to rediscover the real YOU, the calm, capable, confident Self which is seeking unfoldment and expression. Weekends of the kind you describe will not do it, nor will losing yourself in your work, or discussing your dilemma with other frantic friends. You must seek solitude. That is how you will find the power and the sense of direction you need.

Become aware of the presence of God, the consciousness of something higher and greater than your seemingly uncertain self. Find time. Take time. Make time for *meditating, affirming and visualizing the divine Presence in yourself and in your family.* Life is a reflection of your thoughts. Find time to visualize and steer your thoughts into calmer waters and all else will follow.

MB

Question: Please help me to have a will to live! Give me a word that will make me want to go on. I got interested in Unity after my husband left me. Through their teachings I realize now the many, many mistakes I made. I have reaped what I sowed. How can I forgive myself when I drove away the man I love and made hardships for my children? I am full of self-hate. I am not going to get a second chance to prove to him that my thinking has changed. Help me find peace. Give me a word.

D. A.

Answer: I will give you the word, but you must live it. The word is: TRUST! I give it to you because it is already within you, waiting to be expressed. It is speaking through your letter, rising above your complaint, echoing in all you say. It is your word. Begin to live it. Unity will help you live it. TRUST!

Trust that this is your time and your opportunity for spiritual growth and rebirth in body, mind and spirit.

Trust that an all-loving Father has already forgiven you.

Trust that the unfolding days ahead will lead you into new awareness of the true you, strong enough to meet any and all of life's challenges.

Trust that you can rid yourself of self-hate, of destructive, negative thoughts and ruinous complaints.

Trust that the seemingly impossible is always possible and that the "miracle" happens when you prepare yourself in calmness, quietude and gratitude for its happening.

Trust in your capacity for love over hate, faith over fear, strength over weakness, and peace over self-condemnation.

Trust your courage to TRUST in the wisdom, guidance and wonder-working power of God.

MB

Question: I would like to know if psychic phenomena can stir up allergies, as my doctor said. I have witnessed some in this apartment, which stands on the site where a house once burned down. I read Unity and it never bothered me until the doctor, who is Chinese, said, "Get out of there, it is known to stir up allergies!" I feel that I am not getting the right medical care and medicines such as antihistamines cause me to sleep less. Yet if I go any other place, I seem to sleep better. My asthma is superimposed. Good places to live are hard to get.

MRS. C. H.

Answer: The real causes of allergies is still an open question among reputable allergists. Is the cause due to certain substances, such as germs, pollen, food, cats, dogs, feathers or what-have-you, or is it due to hypersensitivity, fear, repugnance, resentment centered in the mind, causing chemical reactions in the body? The evidence suggests that both the environment and the psyche can cause allergic reactions. Proof has been established in both. In answer to your question, I would say it is possible that an aversion to psychic phenomena could stir up allergies in a certain type of mind. So can power of suggestion.

I would certainly choose spiritual teaching above antihistamines or sleeping compounds any day—or night—and would prescribe a year's subscription to the *Daily Word* and to *Unity* magazine for your Chinese practitioner. It would also be a good idea to have your Unity minister or some of your dedicated Unity people come out to your apartment and bless it and you.

MB

7

Of the Strange and Unusual

~~~~~~

Question: While listening to a speaker in her chapel, I noticed a white light around her head and shoulders. With me were two friends. They did not see the aura. In subsequent visits I have not seen it while I was with other companions.

Is it possible that my two friends may have acted as electrodes, or catalysts, to intensify the metaphysical power in me? All three of us have had paranormal experiences, together and separately. What common attributes have persons who experience what is called "extended vision"?

I am aware of a Presence that has become manifest in times of stress. Since retiring from teaching, I am free from worry and have not heard the voice or seen the light. My times of meditation have been irregular. Is there a connection? In my very comfortable retirement home I am surrounded by people, and though I live alone, I have little privacy.

J. L.

Answer: Whenever I receive a letter such as yours (and there are many dealing with visions, auras and altered states of consciousness), I am tempted to say, *"Don't analyze, realize!"* This dictum might be something for you to think about, even though I share your analytical curiosity as to how it all "works."

Extended visions, auric reading, spiritual second sight, heightened perceptivity—most genuine paranormal experiences are not *made* to happen, they just *happen*. Depth analysis often prevents the occurrence of the phenomena. I realize that this kind of reasoning is contrary to that of parapsychological and psychic investigators, but I am looking at the occurrence not from their standpoint, but from yours, and mine.

I know of no reason why we human beings should not anticipate and expect "extended visions" and occasionally witness the emanation of auras, not only from people, but from mountains and lakes and sunsets and sunrises. After all, if the eye of a moth has some twenty-five thousand lenses, each with crystalline cone and nerve-rod, and if each such unit is capable of independent vision and also mosaic vision, shall we not assume that God's human creation also has a chance for experiencing extraordinary phenomena. There *is* a possibility that your friends contribute to your "psychic insight," by virtue of harmonization with you. They may provide a channel of release for your inner vision.

Attend for a moment to the thoughts of writer John C. Lilly: "Compulsion is being trapped in a known psychic reality, a dead-end space. Freedom is in the unknown. If you believe there is an unknown everywhere, in your own body, in your relationships with other people, in political institutions, in the universe, then you have maximum freedom. If you can examine old beliefs and realize they are limits to be overcome, and can also realize you do not need a belief about something you don't yet know anything about, you are free."

Stay free.

MB

Question: Do you believe in UFOs? Do they have any spiritual significance?

E. T.

Answer: I believe that Unidentified Flying Objects exist, even though their existence has never been satisfactorily substantiated or explained.

For some twelve years I served on the board of governors of the National Investigative Committee on Aerial Phenomena (NICAP),

Washington, D.C. The overwhelming majority of the thousands of UFO sightings was explained away as fast-moving unconventional aircraft, weather balloons, meteorites, atmospheric phenomena, subjectivistic visions and so on. However, the residue of unexplained sightings was so authoritative, so well documented that serious, ongoing investigation is more than justified. Currently active in studying all UFO reports (including NICAP data) is a group called Aerial Phenomenon Research Organization, with headquarters in Tucson, Arizona.

The connection of UFOs with religion is largely the result of an attempt by religious enthusiasts to relate apocalyptic and prophetic scriptural references to the mystery and persistence of UFO sightings. I do not go that far, but I am keeping an open mind!

MB

Question: How come nothing new ever happens in the field of religion? Take any other field—electronics, automobiles, styles, even toys—there are always new innovations. In religion and the churches it is always the same old thing.

A. C.

Answer: It is more fitting to compare religion to love and human behavior than to the areas you mentioned. Every individual's discovery and demonstration of the unlimited possibilities of spiritual growth is a break-through, new and innovative.

If you are referring to sensational things, here is one you may have missed: a Swedish doctor, Nils-Olof Jacobson, says that a human soul weighs twenty-one grams (about three-fourths of an ounce). He arrived at this figure by placing terminal patients on extremely sensitive scales. As each one died and the soul left the body, the needle dropped twenty-one grams.

How's that for news!

MB

Question: My question: is there such a thing as witchcraft or any other medium that plays uncanny, unbelievable tricks on people? Let me explain what happened to me. I lost my keys. I searched the house over and over. I looked in every pocket. Two days later I put my hand in my pocket and there were the keys. What do you make of this very strange thing?

T. W.

Answer: By the very nature of my work and research, I am continually running into people with stories such as yours and with experiences as bewildering as the one you describe. Not only that, strange and unusual things keep happening to me! So what can I say in answer to your question, but that there are mysteries inexplicable, happenings extraordinary and circumstances unaccountable.

There may be telekinetic forces at work which we do not fully understand, tricks of the mind we cannot completely comprehend, subjective encounters beyond our powers of explanation and even psychical occurrences not yet fully grasped by the rational mind. It's really not witchcraft. It's phenomena.

About those keys: You may not really have examined that particular pocket as thoroughly as you thought. Someone may have played a trick on you. Are you married? Do you have children?

Up in Canada where we have a cabin, a boy of six wandered away from camp and was lost in the mountains for three days. The search for him was intense and involved many hopeful endeavors, including prayer. On the third morning the boy was found, huddling in the hollow of a tree, unharmed and unafraid. The strange thing about this was that when he wandered off, he had no money. *Now* he had a quarter in his pocket. He didn't have *anything* in his pockets when he strolled away, *now* he had a religious tract that said, "Jesus loves me." I interviewed the boy and must confess that I came to no final conclusion about these circumstances. He even claimed he had had a "guide."

I have a hunch that everyone reading your question has had a mysterious or serendipitous experience to parallel your story about the keys. I am also sure that many readers will ask, "What does MB really believe?" To repeat, I believe it's phenomena. And wouldn't life be dull without it? But *with* it, you must admit, life continues to be phenomenal!

MB

Question: Is there a reason as to why "things" are in the number seven? Seven seas, seven wonders of the world, etc.?

BETTE

Answer: My aging book on occult and esoteric studies tells me that seven is the figure of fate personified. Ask anyone to choose a number between one and ten and chances are the selection will be seven. It is no doubt the most serendipitous member of the numerological family.

There are seven holy sacraments in liturgical churches; seven churches of the Apocalypse; Jesus Christ spoke seven times on the cross; there are seven ministering angels, seven plagues, seven loaves in the basket at the feeding of the multitude. God rested on the seventh day; Joshua marched seven times around the city before the walls came tumbling down; there are seven colors in the rainbow, seven notes in music. There are more references to seven than are known to the seventh son of the seventh son in the light of a seven-stemmed candelabra.

MB

Question: What is meant by the "music of the spheres"? Is this just a saying, or is there something more to it?

C. D.

Answer: There is evidently more to it than merely a catchy phrase, namely, cosmological harmony. Give most of the credit to the Greek philosopher Pythagoras, who apparently heard the music and explained it by saying that the universe is a gigantic monochord, a single cosmic string attached at one end to absolute spirit and at the other to absolute matter. Each planet, as it rushes through space, strikes its particular note, confirming, if you will, what Job described as the morning stars singing together. No doubt Shakespeare had something similar in mind when, in *The Merchant of Venice,* he said, "There's not the smallest orb which thou beholdest but in its motion like an angel sings." What do you say we listen?

MB

Question: I need an answer to something that has been troubling me for twenty-five years. After buying a house, I ran into a financial problem and needed one hundred dollars desperately. My salary was very low. I prayed, as my prayers had often been answered before. This time, no answer, and I was really desperate. That night, at work at a busy hotel's front-office desk, there was nothing on my mind but my need and how to meet the house payment the next day. My prayer became a demand. I clenched my fists and pounded on the front desk: "I've got to have one hundred dollars and I've got to have it now! Not tomorrow, not next week, but right now!"

As I walked out to go to dinner, there was a crisp one-hundred-dollar bill, lying there at my feet in this busy (Reno) hotel lobby. I told the story to my son who is quite religious and he said it was an evil spirit at work. I've told it to religionists of my own faith, and they say I forced an answer and that is wrong and no good can come of it. No good did, in the long run, maybe because I accepted their beliefs. I've been troubled all these years, feeling that I did something evil. What do you think about it?

F. J.

Answer: Will you believe me if I tell you that at one period in my life the same thing happened to me? Not with a hundred dollars but with ten, which, in the days of the depression, seemed like a thousand. I too was desperately in need and had gone into a deserted church to have a lonely prayer. After a while I found myself sobbing a bit and quietly, not frantically, beating the chancel at which I was kneeling and saying: "You can do it, Lord, You can do it! What's ten dollars to YOU?"

When I got outside, I walked to the curb to wait for a bus, though I didn't have a dime in my pocket. And there lay a ten-dollar bill. I picked it up without surprise, said, "Thank You, Lord!" (it being in the days before I learned, "Thank You, Father!"), got on the bus and annoyed the motorman because I had nothing smaller than a ten. He must have thought me quite an affluent financier. Lord knows, I was!

Speaking strictly for myself, both your son and your religious friends were wrong in their estimate of your experience. Better they would have said, as I am saying, "Accept your good as one of the sweet mysteries of life." Many a hundred-dollar bill in Reno or Las Vegas has found its way into worse hands than yours, and if the Lord or any mortal left ten dollars in the grass for me as an answer to prayer, I'm not about to blame it on the devil. If he (Satan) left it there for evil, God meant it for good. "Thank You, Father!"

MB

Question: I was visiting some friends one evening, and while looking at and listening to a girl friend talking, I suddenly was aware of an aura surrounding her head, reaching down over both her shoulders. I watched this for some time and then interrupted her by telling her what I was seeing. She was very startled, as were the other guests. However, after a few minutes she continued her story and I continued to see the aura. The color was soft gold. Is there anything you could tell me about this?

Mrs. J. P.

Answer: Auras, the emanation from what is believed to be the etheric, atomic or "subtle" body, are being reported with increasing frequency. One reason is that people in our age are less inhibited about discussing phenomena of this kind than they once were. It is an age of the growing unity of religion and science, a period that Charles Fillmore foresaw in his writings. Today, scientists are taking a new look at auras, as is attested by recent scientific books, journals, and articles on the subject.

Even dictionary definitions have been upgraded to reflect the new understanding in this enticing field. Webster's New International Second Edition Dictionary now defines *aura* as any subtle, invisible emanation or exhalation from a substance, as the aroma of flowers, hence a supposed emanation conveying mesmeric and similar influences; a distinctive atmosphere surrounding a person; a supposed electric fluid, emanating from an electrified body, and forming a mass surrounding it, called the electrical atmosphere."

Let me share an interesting observation in the auric field. When the Canadian hockey team defeated the Russian team in their final, crucial game in Moscow, a news picture was taken at the peak moment of the Canadian victory. The photograph showed that the members of the Canadian team had auras over their heads. The defeated Russian team did not appear to have these emanations. Some people might say that since the Russian players were obviously Communists, they did not have this etheric glow! But this was not the case. It was ecstasy that created the light among the Canadians, and it was dejection that blocked it out among the beaten players.

Whether the aura is in the eye of the observer or whether it is totally in the object has never been fully determined, but the photographic evidence strongly suggests that it is objective. However, the fact that often only one or two people in a group see an aura—as you did and others in your group did not—again raises the question of whether some people have auric sight and others do not.

MB

8

Of Dreams and Dreaming

~~~~~~

Question: What determines the symbology of dreams?

B. M.

Question: How seriously do you take dreams?

G. S.

Question: Do dreams have any true meaning?

R. J.

Question: I dream quite a bit. One dream that keeps recurring has to do with dogs. I would be greatly interested to know what dreams of this kind signify.

H. F. H.

Answer: These excerpts are representative of many letters dealing with *oneiromancy*—the observation and interpretation of dreams. Aristotle defined dreams as "the direct coming of celestial light to the mind." It is a fascinating field, which I take seriously but not too seriously. I often speculate about it, but I don't pretend to be an expert. I leave my dreams open-ended so they will not lock me in.

Psychologist C. G. Jung suggested that symbolism in dreams is determined primarily by archetypes, or primordial images. There are certain basic instincts, Jung argued, which reveal themselves to the conscious mind by way of imageries. These imageries may be reflections of the collective unconscious mind of all mankind (of which we are a part) and they may also be conditioned by the personal life and experiences of the dreamer.

"I could never agree with Freud," said Dr. Jung, "that a dream is a facade behind which its meaning is hidden. . . . To me dreams are part of nature, which harbours no intention to deceive but expresses something as best it can. Just as a plant grows or an animal seeks its food as best it can."

So-called "primitive man" may have based his belief in a soul or spirit because of the phenomenon of dreaming. After all, here he was sleeping, and there he was hunting or fishing or traveling around as if he were really awake! Can you blame him for believing that he was more than mere "physical" man?

Early occultists looked upon dreams as the work of "mysterious messengers" from outer space or some other etheric realm. Hebrew prophets suggested that dreams came from God and should be interpreted in the light of God's participation in the lives of His people. The prophetic tradition of dream interpretation drew upon symbols characteristic of their time. In the dreams of the Pharaoh, for example, the seven fat cows and the seven lean, which were interpreted by Joseph as seven years of plenty followed by seven years of famine, had as their basis the law and justice of Jehovah. Jacob, dreaming about a ladder rising to the sky, interpreted his dream as a symbol of the rungs of destiny to be traveled by the Jewish people.

Charles Fillmore in his *Talks On Truth* correlated true dreams closely with the work and mission of the Holy Spirit. He used the graphic expression "visions of the night" as a synonym for *dreams,* and reminded us of the scriptural injunction: "If there is a prophet among you, I the Lord make myself known to him in a vision. I speak with him in a dream" (Num. 12:6). Charles Fillmore had "visions of the night" on the level of his high consciousness, and I have a hunch that most of our dreams are channeled or improvised according to the spiritual altitude of *our* thoughts, words and deeds.

This is why I am wary of dream books that suggest stock interpretations and symbols, as if all dreams and dreamers were the same. They aren't. Beware of generalizations designed to fit every situation. The study and meaning of dreams is deeply involved with the reattunement and reconditioning of each individual dreamer.

Furthermore even your diet may determine what you dream, so go easy in your interpretations and your eating. The same key does not open every dream. Symbols are not always clear. They may vary from culture to culture. To the Magi, the Star was a fulfillment of prophecy. To the Romans, it signified a warning. That which is symbolic to the aborigine in his dream time may have a vastly different meaning to a youngster dreaming in Los Angeles.

Since waking, sleeping and dreaming are all states of consciousness, different from one another, yet similar, let's take our dreams in stride, thoughtfully, often with wonder and never forgetting the need for the light touch—or the touch of light.

MB

Question: I heard you say that you give your dreams a "light touch." Does this mean you do not actually believe in them?

A BELIEVER

Answer: How can I help but believe in dreams since I'm a dreamer? But whether to accept dreams as being prophetic, telepathic, intuitive, divine or pathological is another matter. Surely, physiological and psychological conditions affect our dreaming and so, also, does the pad on which I sleep and even the colors of the room in which I do my dreaming.

I definitely believe in dreams. Life would be dull without them. Even daydreams mean more to me than just idle fantasies or mental doodling. We will never know the wonders and miracles dreams have wrought, all the way from Job, who believed that God spoke to mortals during dreams, to Helen Keller, who discovered inner reaches of cognition through her dreaming.

Fascinating circumstances surround the intriguing subject of dreams. Ms. Keller, for instance, sightless and devoid of hearing, once wrote this about dreams: "In sleep I almost never grope. No one needs to guide me. Even in a crowded street I am self-sufficient, and I enjoy an independence quite foreign to my physical life." In one of her dreams she saw a pearl which she held in her hand, although she had never actually seen a pearl or her hand. For studies in depth about the nature, symbols, theories, conscious and unconscious involvements in dreaming we must turn to philosophers such as Plato and Fromm, psychoanalysts like Freud and Jung, to astronomers of the type of Nicolas Flammarion, to occultists, metaphysicians and students in the field of altered states of consciousness.

Despite the profundity of the subject, I still believe in the light touch. For example, during my boyhood when I was studying music, I dreamed incessantly that I was another Paganini or Kreisler, and I accepted these nocturnal visitations all too seriously. They sometimes seem to haunt me now!

But I find it exciting to remember the legendary dream recorded of the incomparable Italian violinist Guiseppe Tartini which resulted in his *Devil's Sonata* or *Devil's Trill.* One day Tartini started to write a composition in a fit of creative passion. Unable to finish it because his fervor ran out, he fell asleep and, in a dream, saw himself wandering aimlessly, desperate and dejected. Suddenly, at the bend in a road, the devil appeared and offered to finish the sonata in exchange for Tartini's soul.

Without any haggling, Tartini accepted the offer and was bedazzled when the devil seized a violin and played a magnificent finale to the unfinished piece. At this, Tartini woke up, jotted down the melody he had heard in the dream, grabbed his violin and played as though his soul were on fire, which it probably was. That is how *The Devil's Sonata* came into being.

To this day, musicians still speak of "Tartini's tones" because they are devilishly—or heavenly—unique. When any two notes are produced as double-stops on the violin, steadily and with great intensity, as in *The Devil's Trill,* a third reverberating note is heard, the vibration of which is the difference between the two double-stops. Tartini insisted that a double-stop on a violin is not perfectly executed unless the throbbing shadow of the third note can be heard.

Even in this concept of the shadow tone there seems to be some sort of hidden message about the art of dreaming, but in order to fully understand, let's sleep on it.

MB

9

Of Faith and Futility

~~~~~~

Question: Do you think there is a specific purpose in each of our many mistakes and the subsequent difficulty it brings? In other words, although we are free to make mistakes, are the consequences of our mistakes already taken into account for an ultimate balancing or canceling out by infinite intelligence? Is this a fruitless line of inquiry?

M. S.

Answer: Johannes Brahms once said, "There are occasions in my work of composing which convince me that the wrong note was necessary for me to find my way to the right note." The implication seems to be that purpose and growth are lurking in many of our seeming mistakes.

That mistakes bring difficulties, as you suggest, may simply mean they represent necessary rungs in the ladder of development. Unless we have reached the spiritual or psychic stature of a Brahms or a Bach (Johann Sebastian, that is), how many wrong notes do we need before we arrive at the goal toward which the experience was directed?

As to your question about the consequences of our mistakes being already taken into account for an ultimate balancing: I have learned something about this from friends who play the stock market. I know very little about the "big board," but my friends tell me that the market is not really erratic, it's mystical. It foresees, foretells and often foreordains the seemingly unconscious direction and thinking of the social, national and international mind. It anticipated the end of the Vietnam war, took it into account, reflected the effect long before the actual culmination of this dragged-out affair. When the good news of the war's end came, many stock market amateurs predicted that the market would go wild. But the seasoned analysts knew that the event had been absorbed and neutralized long before "Peace with honor" actually came.

This neutralizing process, it seems to me, also occurs in our involvement with ourselves. Infinite Intelligence is onto us long before we anticipate the effect or influence of our thoughts and deeds. The prayer we pray is not always answered today, nor even tomorrow. It may have been answered yesterday and already have been canceled out. The amateur prayer will not believe this, and that is the difference between him and the seasoned prayer.

I am not talking about a Wall Street kind of God (God forbid). I am merely saying that on heaven's "big board," (by which I mean the Book of Life), it is not your stock that is judged, it is you.

For an understanding of all this, the purely rational person is of little help. We must go to the mystics. Like Brahms. Or Jacob Boehme. Boehme once explained it thus:

"I saw and comprehended the Being of all Beings. . . . I saw the original and primal existence of this world and of all creatures. Within myself I perceived creation entire, in its order and movement. I saw first the divine world, that of the angels and of paradise, second, the darkened world, the fiery realm and third, this world around us, visible and tangible, as an issue and expression of the two inner, eternal, hidden worlds. Moreover, I comprehended the whole being and reason of Good and Evil."

And there was the sublime mystic William Blake, to whom a friend complained that he was having a round of bad luck and felt deserted of God. Blake turned to his wife Catherine and said: "That's just the way things go with us, too, don't they? There are weeks that the visions forsake us. What do we do then, Kate?" And Catherine replied, "We kneel down and pray, Mr. Blake." It's really not a fruitless line of inquiry at all!

MB

Question: I believe I understand God as Principle. I also understand how God individualized Himself in us personally through Christ. God, although universal, is ours through Christ, the Son.

Now, if Principle is law and a blind force in motion, how can God be "loving"? I believe that the law is good and that there is no situation in which good (God) cannot be found. My difficulty lies in compromising law and a personal love.

If God is all and only good, how can God know about our personal problems and deal with us lovingly? I believe He does, but I believe in faith. Can you explain it?

MRS. R. R. R.

Answer: Before we get into this, let's add another ingredient to your concept of "God as Principle." Let's add *life.* I know you imply this by saying that God "individualized Himself," but I want to be sure that we understand Principle as *life,* law and love. It might even help us to take a few deep breaths and say: "I recognize God as *life!* Thank You, Father!"

When we truly recognize God's life in us as our life in Him and extend this recognition to all life, then law and love take on a new and larger meaning. We realize that though we may consider God as personalized, it is more correct to say that He is manifested. Personalization implies division. Manifestation suggests unity.

What I am getting at is the necessity of making central the recognition that God is not fragmented. Forgive the repetition, but He is *not* individualized—He is manifested, expressed, revealed. Life is God's first and greatest creation, and law and love are duty-bound to sustain it, even when it doesn't seem that way to us.

Think along this line and your questions will answer themselves. You will see that God's law isn't a "blind force in motion" but is consistently interacting with life and love. Love is constantly interacting with life and law, and life with love and law. God must certainly be a good parent.

Everyone, at some time or other, has been stumped by what we call "acts of God." I mean tragic occurrences which seem contrary to our idea of divine law. They often seem callous to the value of life, devoid of love and in conflict with even our human idea of true law or justice.

Yet at this very point, when we stand face to face with one of these inexorable happenings, the blow can be softened, though not always fully understood, if we remember that God as Principle is life, law and love. This, as you indicate, is where faith comes in to play its phenomenal role. It forces us to believe that Principle as law is not blind force in motion, but something beyond our human, cortical capability to understand. And somehow faith causes our will to respond to the will of God. Or, as Paul said, "Faith is the assurance of things hoped for, the conviction of things not seen."

Your letter conveys your own confidence and understanding of this when you say that you believe the law is good and that good (God) is in every situation.

It is easier to believe it if we keep *life* in mind as part of the Principle. Law and love are surely always on the side of life when we live in God's jurisdiction. In this respect, your creed is my creed, too, and if I ever stop believing it, I am out of business!

MB

Question: I have been a "Truth" student for almost fifty years. I have gone through correspondence courses and also had a number of articles published in magazines. I love metaphysical teachings and I study my Bible using Charles Fillmore's *Metaphysical Bible Dictionary* and get so much out of it.

Right now I am a member of the Methodist Church. I like the Methodist Church because of the liberal view they allow members, many of whom read "Truth" literature.

It seems to me, though, that most churches teach that our daily problems and challenges are "crosses" that we must bear as Christians. One of our pastors recently said in a sermon that our daily challenges are just part of being a Christian, and that the difficult jobs or challenges which we take on voluntarily are our "crosses." How would you interpret this?

H. F.

Answer: Your question reminded me of the phrase, "Carry the cross," which as a boy I heard many times in our orthodox Protestant church. My mother frequently used this saying, and we had a neighbor, an elderly Catholic woman stooped in pain, who said she was "carrying the cross for Jesus." Her name was Sabina. The cross she carried was her feeling of guilt and her fear of God's judgment because years ago she had been divorced. She was still doing constant penance and often put pebbles in her shoes to cause her physical pain, the better to show God that she was willing to carry His cross and suffer for righteousness' sake.

Though this may sound like something out of the Middle Ages (when a certain masochism was tantamount to the invocation of God's pity), there are, as you indicate, people in our day who insist that they must walk the Via Dolorosa for Jesus' sake. I am not condemning them or making light of what may be a deeply ingrained conviction. A Penitente boy once told me, after he had flagellated himself during a Holy Week ceremony, that "you cannot understand what Jesus suffered until you suffer as He did."

Crucifying one's life in this way is, however, a misplaced belief and a perversion of the true *Christian* meaning of the cross, which sees in it a symbol of exaltation, triumph and magnificent overcoming. If Jesus Christ was lifted up so that a dark Good Friday became a brilliant Easter morning, let us all be lifted with Him in love and peace and leave the cross silently silhouetted against the spiritual sky. Most cross carrying is false modesty trimmed with a touch of self-righteousness.

Your minister perhaps meant that if we volunteered to meet our challenges with courage and if we took our often tasteless jobs in stride, our so-called "burdens" could be lightened and our attitudes improved. Or he might have meant that we should always carry our crosses valiantly, as the early Crusaders were pledged to do. Or he could have had in mind the refining power that comes of accepting our duties as divine commands.

Why not ask him sometime just what he *did* mean? Too many preachers leave too much unclear.

MB

Question: Who and what are demons? The Bible speaks of a demon as a disembodied personality looking for a physical body to live in and make of that body a devil, and these embodied personalities cause all the crimes and sins. One illustration is where the demons entered some animals and all the animals rushed into the water and drowned. I just hope I never encounter one of them!

Mrs. F. C.

Answer: You won't encounter them if you keep yourself in good physical condition and stay on the side of love and truth! Another thing to remember is that the Bible and other ancient books of wisdom abound in symbols, allegories and metaphors which were part of the idiom of their time but which are not necessarily part of ours.

Possession by an evil spirit was once considered the cause of many illnesses, both mental and physical. This is no longer true today, though some people would like to put the blame for their misdeeds and poor physical condition on some evil spirit instead of taking the responsibility upon themselves.

What we refer to today as germs and viruses were once considered to be demons, devils and powers of darkness. What we label "mental illness" was once construed as possession and witchcraft, even in the United States as late as 1776. Many people who are now treated by psychiatrists would have been sent to exorcists in the Middle Ages.

Not that we moderns are immune to the notion of demonic possession! Your letter indicates, as do other letters that come to me, that there is still lively speculation that there are entities all around us waiting to pounce the moment we give them half a chance. One of the most popular movies several seasons ago was based upon the theme of exorcism, and it proved that the subject of demon possession is deep-seated in the collective unconscious (the thought realm) of millions of Americans.

Demons in Biblical times were considered to be "unclean spirits." Demons in our time are unclean thoughts, evil, conniving, ungodly passions, dark, sinister motives, warped thinking, egomaniacal ambitions, duplicity, insensitivity to good, ignorance and rejection of divine law and so on.

Metaphysical teaching will give you an insight into the deeper meaning and motivation of these spectacular personifications of today's "powers of darkness." Enlightened, liberated, spiritually minded people recognize themselves as manifestations of God, and they know that the Godness, this goodness which is their true life, overcomes any destructive influence by means of the *counterpower* of belief in a God of love and truth. There is nothing to fear.

MB

Question: I almost cringe when I ask this question and I even know you understand. But this is a principle and I dare ask. I give my tenth gladly, joyfully and expectantly. For three years I did this and in those three years I had a major operation, my husband lost his job, his drinking is worse, and I will not give you a litany of my circumstances. I give you just my sincere, questioning, "Why?" I still give. I searched myself deeply to see if there are any misgivings or fears, and I think there are none. Is there something I overlook? This is my question. I dare not ask anyone else.

K. M. H.

Answer: Many letters like yours reach me regularly. So don't cringe!

In most of these letters, as in yours, I see a disappointment that deserves consideration. This is to say, a person tithes and then is surprised because of sickness or a marital problem or a discouraging social situation or some other annoying circumstance. Please do not misunderstand me: all of life is surely interrelated and the more completely life is integrated, the more one should expect complete good fortune.

But tithing is not necessarily going to keep your husband from drinking. If he resents your tithing, it may even be driving him to drink, or he may be using your "religiosity" as an excuse for his actions. Also, there are laws of health which operate independently of tithing and are as immutable as the law of tithing which insists that "as we give so shall we receive." As we give attention to the body by way of nutritional eating, exercise and discipline, health improves and destructive habits, such as excessive drinking, are more easily overcome. In all the seeming unrelatedness of life, there is also a close relatedness.

You say you give your tenth "gladly, joyfully and *expectantly.*" For the sake of an adventure in faith, try giving it "gladly, joyfully and *forgettingly.*" Tithing is not a lottery; it is a spiritual act. It is not a giving to be *getting,* but a giving to be *growing* in spirit and Truth.

Thank you for writing just as you did. No cringing! We are all on the quest together. We all have our moments of questioning. The "why" is universal. The "ifs" and "buts" run like a knotted thread throughout Scripture, and even Jesus was not spared His moments of spiritual struggle and deepened thought.

You are now at a point of spiritual growth; I sense it in your letter. I read it between the lines. God's purpose for your life is spiritual fulfillment. I believe in bowing to His will, in learning to submit, in trusting in His love. But I also believe in learning more about His laws and rules for life in the field of health, in person-to-person relationships, in stewardship and so on. Seek all this in meditation, in study and in sincere spiritual pursuits. Raise your sights to total life! Try it for a while and write me again.

MB

Question: Why is it that with all I believe, with all my faith and even with a certain amount of success, I am still overcome by a sense of futility and incompleteness? What I mean is, I don't seem able to get with it.

EDGAR H.

Answer: Your lines reflect a mood and spirit I often find among college students. Like you, many of them take a dim view of things. Others despair of ever finding meaningful values. Some are loners, copping out, searching, drifting, sure they will never find anyone who really understands them, distrusting teachers, preachers, politicans and society generally—at least, they try to give this impression.

I often wonder whether one factor in this malaise, over and above its many sociological and psychological aspects, is that, in our attempt to adjust to a role in life or to a certain norm of experience, what we really wish for, and dream about, is something not reducible to mere *human* experience. We are looking for something above and beyond this, perhaps something beyond human attainment.

Every material achievement, to be fully satisfying, needs to take place in the context of a nonmaterial, spiritual world view, and this need cannot be compensated by money or even appreciation, insight and compliments, sincere though they be. What we really want and need to satisfy ourselves is something deeply validating within us. But because our idealism is usually superior to our accomplishments, we have what you describe as a "sense of futility and incompleteness."

Actually, you wouldn't want it any other way, would you really? Isn't there a certain joy in your loneliness and a subtle sense of expanding life and fulfillment concealed in your complaint?

If things were as "perfect" as you wanted them to be, what would you do with your faith that wants them to be even better? Cheer up, you're a fellow spirit along the way of the quest—and probably a Sagittarian!

MB

Question: I am lost, bewildered and very lonely. I have discovered that the seeker must walk alone, and it is hard to walk alone, especially when what you have thought was a light in the darkness is only a flicker from the distant beacon that glows further on. I've discovered so many religions and so many paths that lead to God, but not the path that I can walk with confidence, knowing my path will not end. I need a path that never ends, that doesn't stop and make me commit myself to the point that I must deny the existence of other lights. In my path of discovery I have found more likenesses among the religions than differences, and that these differences are manmade, not God-made. As I search I stumble more frequently, and each time the getting up again becomes more difficult because I feel so alone in my searching.

G. A.

Answer: You are not alone. You are walking the path of Spirit with us, or we with you. There are many more who, though they have found so much in the way of Truth, still feel the loneliness and a sense of divine discontent, often telltale signs of spiritual growth and spiritual understanding. Even Jesus had His lonely moments and once stood weeping over the city.

As for the light, it is already in us and we cannot move toward it or away from it because God is that light. You say you need a path that never ends. You have it. I have it. So let's be grateful. Wouldn't it be boring to end up in a cul-de-sac or in a parking lot?

There is no true search without discovery. The ultimate awareness is that the quest and the question are in themselves the way.

You say you stumble. Don't we all at times, especially when we try to move too fast and insist on doing our own moving instead of letting ourselves be moved. Expect great and good things to happen in your life. Make it an adventure. And do let us hear from you again.

MB

Question: If it is true that we reap what we sow and the power of our word is dynamic, what happens to a Christian, in professional life an actor or actress, who is chosen for the part of the villain or murderer or robber (as the case may be) in a play? All the spiritual laws of love and progressive good, etc., are broken by the spoken word and physical actions required in these parts, are they not? This being the case, what is the effect of the broken spiritual law in this instance? Are the seeds of the evil words sown by an "imaginary" evil character reaped by the unsuspecting Christian, or what? Or can we all play games with words and pretend we didn't really say the awful things about our next-door neighbor, etc.? Maybe one can't be an actor and a Christian at the same time!

PAULINE D.

Answer: Surely, all the world's a stage, as Shakespeare said, and the men and women (kids, too) are merely players!

You need not go to the legitimate theater to find Christians playing a role or wearing masks. You need not go to a show to find people who assume the roles of villains and mouth their angry lines—that happens in even the best-regulated families—and the words return, bearing their weight of retribution with them. Of course, words spoken to curse often come back to bless, as in the famous case of Saul of Tarsus, who condemned the Christians and became one of their most devoted defenders.

The power of our words is actually a matter of consciousness. I once wrote an article about a man who for years played the Christ in a Passion Play. He told me how playing his role had transformed and deepened his character. Yet the man who played the part of Judas was also softened and transformed (for good) by his characterization of the betrayer, because he entered into the agony and conflict of Iscariot caught in the divine drama. And aren't we all so caught at times?

In this respect, it is our identification with our deepest (or highest) self that brings back the "karma" of our lives. When you scream at a friend, "You're really impossible!" because you secretly love him so much, it is not the words but the thought behind the words, the spirit behind the thought and the Self behind the spirit that plays the leading part in the final denouement.

You see, there is a communication barrier between the self and the non-self or, if you wish, between the objective and the subjective self, a barrier fully as great as that between two people. There are times when words fail to provide an effective medium for our deepest feelings. This may be why, in the experience of the Baptism of the Holy Spirit, the language is often either a gibberish, an ecstatical outburst, or an unknown tongue (glossolalia). Words not explicable are often more meaningful than words we understand.

Professional actors have a way of simultaneously being and not-being. They can play the part of a stammerer without becoming a habitual stammerer, or the role of a paraplegic without losing control of their bodies, or they can, when called upon, be laughing behind their tears.

To answer your first question last: according to all great religious teachers, we *do* reap what we sow. The only difficulty with this is that we sometimes do not learn to recognize the nature of the seeds until we have done the planting and the harvesting. So it is with words. And so with life. And that's what makes it all so interesting.

MB

Question: I was shocked at the death of Kathryn Kuhlman. These things bother me. When they can heal others why can't they heal themselves? How old was she and what did she die of?

AVA M.

Answer: Because your question came as a telephone call rather than a letter, following the Forest Lawn Memorial Park (Los Angeles) funeral of this noted evangelist, it indicates your anxiety for a fixed opinion about the things that bother you. As is the case with most spiritual healers, or "faith healers," Miss Kuhlman used the approach: "I cannot heal you, I can only point the way. I lead you to The Great Physician and the rest is up to Him and you." Yet the public's impression is that the evangelist is *the* healer, just as the impression persists that the physician heals you, when in fact nature does the job, or that drugs heal you, when they merely assist nature, or, more often than not, do not! Those who heal are channels for healing and have never, to my knowledge, professed physical immortality for themselves or for those they heal.

Hidden by the sensationalism surrounding the Kuhlman services were a number of features: the powerful prayer ministry of thousands who believed in her and whose consciousness contributed to her power; the foundation she established in Pittsburgh, where I interviewed her long ago and where help was afforded to the handicapped, to drug addicts and to the needy; and the missionary work which included several foreign countries.

She died in Tulsa two months after open-heart surgery. She was said to have been sixty-six. Born a Methodist, she was ordained as a Baptist minister. Her following, though basically consisting of conservative, fundamentalist Christian groups—evangelistic, Pentecostal—also contained many non-Christians as well. Her largest and most consistent audiences were those who greeted her each month in the Los Angeles Shrine Auditorium. For ten years in a row her followers filled the seven thousand seats and many more were turned away. But even more far-reaching were her TV specials.

She was a phenomenon of our age, but she need not be referred to as the last great faith healer of our time because there is that in the human heart which always seeks a renactment of the miracle of healing attributed to Christ.

MB

Question: About five years ago I took my nine-year-old boy with some friends to a church revival. My boy was frightened by the words of the minister, who said that sinners would suffer eternal punishment by frying in hell. My boy had never heard words like that. Isn't God love, and didn't He create all for the good of His children?

E. E. C.

Answer: There is something wrong with a ministry that instills fear and fright instead of faith and forgiveness. It has well been said that "there is something wrong with a religion—or a religionist—that frightens a child." An understanding of the concepts of love and truth should set things in their proper perspective.

MB

10

Of Prayer and Meditation

~~~~~~

Question: How does one meditate and what does one think of or about during meditation? As I understand it, to meditate, one thinks deeply, but just exactly about what and how? I pray and try to meditate, and the more I try to meditate, the more my thoughts fly from one thing to another. They get more cluttered and crowded and I am more frustrated and more anxious than ever before. Should I try TM?

<div align="right">

MRS. M. T.

</div>

Answer: Your question states a case repeated over and over in letters that come to me. "The more I try to meditate or pray, the more my thoughts fly from one thing to another" is almost a stock phrase. Then comes the question, "Should I try TM (Transcendental Meditation)?" Or, "Should I try yoga or Zen or some other method?" As a reply to these sincere and searching letters like yours, my research and experience keep saying, "The answer to your question is in you."

I have no doubt that TM would help you. It is part of the TM technique to provide, through means of a word or mantra or inner focal point, a mental mooring to which one consistently returns when extraneous thoughts intrude. To learn the technique you would have to take the course, or at least follow the instructions in Maharishi's books.

There are, however, things you can do immediately, by yourself, if you are willing to clear up several obvious misconceptions. For one thing, meditation and/or prayer require a discipline involving *total* life, *total* living. Forget about formal meditation or prayer for a moment. Can you sit quietly relaxed and think about a concept like love or peace or beauty or serenity without getting frustrated? If you can't, practice until you can. If you can, you are ready for meditation and prayer.

I know that this kind of discipline works. I had a friend who for a long time was harassed and frustrated. Whenever his life seemed completely frazzled, he would say, "I've got to pray!" So he would rush into prayer, but his prayers were no different than his overall frantic life style. Finally, discovering that the answer to his problems lay in *himself*, he learned not to be calmed by praying, but to pray by being calm.

I wish we had space to explore this subject at greater length, but you see how life is! We must learn to adjust! Let me simply add that when you anticipate the answer to your question in TM or any form of eastern meditation, you are embarking on a trail which leads you right back to the depth meditation of the Christian path. All *true* meditation is *transcendental.* There is great value in studying other than specifically Christian methods, but no religion, no faith, no philosophy has a monopoly or corner on Truth. They are all present aspects of and insights into universal consciousness. Investigate, work with them as you wish, take courses in meditation or whatever, but remember that *the answer to your question is in you.*

MB

Question: I would like your opinion about the value of "Guided Meditation." What is your understanding of it?

J. J. B.

Answer: Guided Meditation, which seems to be growing in popularity, takes many forms. I interpret it as a journey in mind and spirit under the direction of a wayshower or pathfinder. For example, say you have a problem that needs solution. Let's imagine that I am serving as your guide. I would ask you to sit quietly with me in meditation and prayer. We would seek guidance and affirm that an answer to the challenge will be given. We would close our eyes. I would be led to say:

"We are now walking along a beautiful forest trail. It is spring. The scent of spring is in the air. The sun filtering through the overhanging trees forms lovely patterns of light and shadow around us. We are walking into the sun, but it is gentle and easy on the eyes. Light is directing us.

"Now we are entering a lovely appointed place where there is a small, rippling waterfall so gentle that it makes only a whispering, musical sound. The sunlight playing on the water is shimmering silver, peaceful, restful, quiet. It looks as if these moss-covered stones were put here just for us. Let's sit down."

Our unfolding scenario would continue. We would follow our guidance, which would include my directing your attention to a teacher who steps into the scene. After describing the teacher and making us all feel en rapport, I would say, "He asks you to tell him your problem. He is eager to hear all about it. Go ahead and tell him."

You would then recount to him, aloud if only you and I are together, silently if our Guided Meditation is conducted with a participating group, your story, your thoughts, your concerns. With candor and openness you would unburden your mind and heart as we sit together in this meditation fantasy which has, by now, become very real.

When you have finished reporting to the teacher, I would say, "Now the teacher has something to say to you. Listen carefully to every word and take to heart what is being said."

You listen and relate aloud what you *feel,* what you imagine you are *hearing,* what you *sense* the teacher has to say to you. You have actually, of course, turned the problem over to an inner consciousness of the divine Presence, and out of this interplay a solution frequently springs.

We would then return over the sunlit path to our starting point. Grateful in prayer for our adventure in Guided Meditation, we would affirm that we have been supplied with new insight and, hopefully, a solution to your problem.

MB

Question: I am wondering what your thoughts might be on an idea that keeps nudging me to action. For some time now I have had the thought, "Are we using Jesus as a middleman between ourselves and God?" So often our prayers are aimed at Jesus the Christ instead of being taken directly to God, who is the real source of all we need eternally. I hope you understand that I am not trying to be blasphemous.

MARIE A.

Answer: Your question has bugged many people ever since the deification of Jesus began with Peter's statement, "You are the Christ, the Son of the living God." This dictum, confirmed by Paul's contention that Jesus preexisted with God and took on human form, put the seal upon the incarnation of Christ or the "Logos," as theologians say. Viewed in *this* light, those who pray to Jesus the Christ feel they are praying not to an intermediary but directly to God. To them, Christ *is* God.

Many orthodox Christians who are of this opinion make no distinction between Jesus, the historical figure, and the Christ, second Person of the Trinity. When they pray "in the name of Jesus," they have in mind not only a highly skilled moral teacher but, again, God Himself.

In your letter you reminded us that Jesus said, "I do nothing on my own authority but speak thus as the Father taught me." This would suggest that the power awakened through prayer is the God-consciousness within each individual. Whether this can be quickened by praying "in the name of Jesus" or "in the name of Jesus Christ" depends upon the individual's interpretation and conviction.

If you are interested in pursuing the theological controversies on this subject, read any of the many books on Christology or refer to a religious encyclopedia under this title. But by all means pursue the topic using your own "primary sources," by which I mean the deep insight into your own convictions and whatever revelation you feel has sincerely been entrusted to *you.*

Each person is a valid recipient for God's light somewhere along the way!

MB

Question: Can you explain what is meant by the provocative expression "entering into the silence"?

Y. F.

Answer: In Western terminology "entering into the silence" commonly means finding the point of stillness at which prayer, meditation or spiritual reflection reaches an unawareness of everything but the awareness of oneness with God.

Oriental philosophy has a similar, more mystical explanation. The silence is the "eye of the hurricane," the quiet, abated center of the storm within which no motion is evident. The "eye" is what makes the hurricane possible, and the hurricane makes the eye.

MB

Question: Do you think meditation, with its promise of renewal (physical and spiritual), will someday replace the human's need for sleep? I am one who would love to get by on much less sleep than what I need now, which is eight hours. Is it worth a try to get into meditation more than I have been doing, twenty minutes a day? Thank you for your kindness and valuable time. Unity teachings and wonderful people like you have done wonders in my life and in helping me to help others.

BARB K.

Answer: Apart from the psychological fact that the more you are impelled by a specific drive, a creative will to achieve or by an all-consuming love, the less sleep is required, there is the meditative discipline about which you inquire. I think most meditation is too superficial, too formalized and mechanized, too concerned with adjustment to the outer world, to help us reach the goal we seek. When you talk about meditating twenty minutes a day, it is already an indication of a constructive approach. We can hardly, effectively, meditate by the clock. Meditation is by the spirit, and we often stop meditation about the time we are just "getting into it."

According to mystical belief, true meditation, in its deepest sense, brings the "desire body" into a higher spiritual awareness. Most "avatars" and "yogis" who are truly dedicated to self-realization emphasize that extreme discipline is required, bodily appetites must be curbed, the sex force controlled, the total disposition of the person heightened. Only then, because there is less conflict in daily living and, therefore, less damage in body, mind and spirit to be restored, will less sleep be required.

MB

Question: I had been sick and off the job for nearly three weeks. I am not a very medically minded gal and decided to work this out on my own. I believe in prayer, and I prayed. When I got back to the office a woman said to me: "I knew you'd get better. I was praying for you." Do you think her prayers helped, even though I didn't know she was praying? How does prayer work? If God loves me and wants me to be well, can't He do it without someone praying and making me feel obligated to her, when I didn't even ask her to pray?

L. T.

Answer: Several years ago, while I was on a round-the-world trip, letters from people with prayer requests were held up at my office. I never saw the letters, yet I received several notifications from these same people thanking me because their prayers had been answered. I concluded that the power for answered prayer is as much in the sincerity of the *asking* as in another's attention to the request. If you have both, however, you should have double the power!

Of course, as you say, you did not ask the woman to pray for you. Nonetheless, the power of prayer is so mystical, and the secret signal running through life so subtle, that we are dealing with mysteries on many fronts. What we do know, however, and what we have come to appreciate more and more, is that in-depth prayer or a heartfelt request for prayer or even an innate longing for prayer—which you may have had—sets in motion emanations that free us from restrictive forces and that reach out (or in) to influence the object of our praying.

It is not the words we use but the depth of our awareness that generates prayer's power. This is not to deny that there is "power in the word," but the true emanation takes place at a spiritual or psychic level beyond words and above verbalization. Your coworker could have reached out to you, though you did not necessarily reach out to her.

God answers prayer by means of our tuning in to His cosmic center, which is a point of stillness within us. There are definitely levels of consciousness and graded force fields by means of which prayer tunes in to the higher octaves of those universal attributes love, compassion and insight.

It would be interesting to find out: (a) what prompted your coworker to pray for you; (b) how she prayed; (c) what words or expressions or aspirations she employed; (d) what emanations or as-surance she felt during her acts of prayer. Why not talk to the woman? Who knows, someday you may be inspired to pray for her, and will very likely do it without even being asked!

MB

Question: In a recent issue of *Unity* magazine someone wrote, "Do not pray for someone's particular need unless you are asked to do so." This puzzles me because I always include in my prayers mothers of little children, doctors, nurses, technicians and all who are in positions of leadership. Surely that can't be wrong. Or is it?

SELMA N.

Answer: Prayers promote and project power. The power of prayer touches and changes people. The Unity quotation was undoubtedly a warning that our prayers should not cross the wave length of some-one whose needs we might not fully know. For example, consider a woman who is very lonely. At least so she seems to us. So we put her on our prayer list and begin praying and affirming that she will get a man. We even drop hints that we are treasure-mapping and praying for just the right man for her. She hears of this "divine scheme" and tells us: "Forget it. I've had my fill of men. All I want is a pet of some kind. A cat or a poodle will do very well, and when I've decided what to get, I'll take care of it. Please call off your prayers." A facetious example? No. This actually happened. We *can* intrude too far into the lives of others. There *are* points at which we infringe upon the dignity and freedom of those we ambitiously seek to help.

To bless the world, to remember professional people in prayer, as you do, to feel a sense of oneness with all who serve, with peo-ple of all walks of life, cultures, creeds and colors is good not only for the power of prayer that goes out from you, but equally con-structive for the power that returns to you. It is a way of enlarg-ing your life, of pushing back your horizons, of getting a broader overview of God's great scheme of things. To bless others is to be blessed.

I even consider it valid and vital, for those who are sensitive and who truly care, to include nature and nature's "little people" (ani-mals) in a prayer blessing, as the Psalmist and other writers of scrip-ture have done, or as poet Margaret Wise Brown did when she said:

Dear Father, hear and bless
Thy beasts and singing birds;
And guard with special tenderness
Small things that have no words.

MB

11

Of Words to Live By and Living Words

~~~~~~

Question: What do you think of the bumper stickers that say: "If you need help, ask God. She'll help you!"?

W. W.

Answer: There is a growing feeling that God should be recognized and represented as androgynous, that is, containing the qualities of both male and female. This belief did not originate with the modern Women's Liberation Movement; it has been around a long time, even before the beginning of the Christian era. But today there is a determined revival of the androgynous concept, and in some churches, the term "Father-Mother God" is being used in prayers and meditations.

The bumper sticker you refer to is, however, a bad parody, a put-on and misses the point. A free car wash should take care of it.

MB

Question: Being ninety-plus years, I cannot read any more except for large print. I have twice come across this quotation and it puzzles me: "The glory which I had with thee before this world was made."

From many trips to the planetarium on 86th Street, New York City, I know that there are many millions of worlds whirling around. So, why "this world"?

Mrs. H. E.

Answer: I must confess that at first the phrase, as you stated it, lured me off on a false scent. I felt I had heard it before and suggested to a librarian who frequently works with me that it sounded like something out of Tennyson or Browning or Blake. We even speculated that it might represent a cry of lament from those disillusioned with the current state of affairs and contemplating the gap between ideals and accomplishments, or the call of those who glimpse that they have strayed a bit from the glory of their divine origin.

But suddenly, challenged and chagrined, I realized it was a phrase straight out of the Good Book! Sure enough, there it was, tucked away in John, chapter 17, Jesus' introductory words to the chapter commonly referred to as "Christ's Prayer for His Own":

> I glorified thee on earth, having accomplished the work which thou gavest me to do; and now, Father, glorify thou me in thy own presence with the glory which I had with thee before the world was made.

We see how a quotation clears itself when put back into its proper context, like a jewel returned to its rightful setting. Commentaries on this passage in orthodox sources, such as the *Interpreter's Bible* and similar references, will hardly reveal the deeper meaning here implied. For this, we must go to metaphysical insights which explain that, as Christ was one with the Father, so is everyone who recognizes that the spiritual consciousness in each person's self is the spirit of Christ reborn.

Today, with the impact of liberalized thought and the contribution of philosopher-scientists such as Teilhard de Chardin, we have come to recognize the value of the opinion that *the Christ energy in us is also the Christic energy in the universe.* In other words, all is God and God *is* all.

Your quotation reads, "The glory which I had with thee before *this* world was made." The word *this* may be throwing you off. There is no *this* world and *that* world, there is only *the* world.

There is a great lesson here. Haven't we all had the experience of suddenly finding ourselves with a *this* world on our hands? I mean, a world of problems and challenges, because we fragmented God's *one* world? In that one world—that is to say, in *the* world—the light and darkness are alike to God and, through spiritual understanding, will also become alike to us and help us in glorifying this Creative Power through deepened perception.

In other words, by reflecting God's glory through unity and love, by seeing God in nature no less than in humankind, we gain a new perception of a divine heritage which was ours, too, before *the* world was made.

I especially appreciated your reference to your visits to the planetarium. As we stand, balanced so beautifully on our tilted, spinning, spaceship Earth, it is truly fabulous to feel that the other millions of galaxies in the boundless universe are also part of God's one world, *Star Wars* and all!

MB

Question: This morning while thoughtfully eating breakfast, I happened to think of a dear, departed friend and a trend of thought came unbidden into my mind. The phrase "reward in heaven" was tied intimately into my thoughts of those who have died. Is it possible, if all is Mind, that our thoughts can give extra warmth and substance to those in another realm (heaven)? Could this go back to the beginning of humanity and add value to all those who have brought us this far? Is it, in a selfish way, a reason to be the best person we can be here on earth?

I am sixty-five, a retired schoolteacher, married, widowed, remarried, mother of four. For years my basic belief has been (as you have often said) to do the best I can, then turn the rest over to God. I am not even sure of my feelings about Christ, although I love Him for what He represents. Also, would you recommend several books that would straighten out my thoughts on my way to Truth?

V. B. K.

Answer: It has been said, "Faith means belief in something concerning which doubt is theoretically possible." That is how I feel about convictions in the field of interconscious communication.

Since we speculate that "Mind is all and all is Mind (God)," and inasmuch as we have faith in some form of immortality, why should we have doubts about our continued close relationship with the departed? Why should we question that we are all interwoven into the oneness of all humankind? This is not a matter of spiritualism or psychism but, rather, an awareness and a perceiving of, and an adventure into, the mystery of life itself.

Your speculation that our thoughts mingle with other thoughts, or the thoughts of others, thereby adding "warmth and substance" to total life, is a precious overview of how closely the family of God is united.

Practical Christianity is best understood at this point: by being the best person we can be here on earth we add to the sum of goodness everywhere, eventually causing the sum of the component parts to be greater than the whole. It is all very wonderful. I am happy that you ate your breakfast "thoughtfully" because eating in a rush rarely allows such extrastellar communication as you reported.

For supplementary sources, I recommend you read as many Unity publications as you can, including, of course, *Lessons in Truth* by H. Emilie Cady and read Teilhard de Chardin's *Phenomenon of Man.* May I assume that you have a copy of my book *The Power of Perception?*

MB

Question: What is meant by the term *cure of souls?*

A. A.

Answer: The term is commonly associated with the priestly and pastoral duties of the clergy in liturgical churches, who, through the administration of the sacraments, counseling, ritual and prayer, seek to bring peace and assurance to the spiritually troubled parishioners concerned with the salvation of their souls.

MB

Question: Who wrote the poem you often quote, "All Roads That Lead to God Are Good"?

E. M.

Answer: Ella Wheeler Wilcox.

> "All roads that lead to God are good;
> What matters it, your faith or mine;

Both center at the goal divine
Of love's eternal brotherhood.

"A thousand creeds have come and gone;
  But what is that to you or me?
  Creeds are but branches of a tree,
The root of love lives on and on.

"Though branch by branch proves withered wood,
  The root is warm with precious wine;
  Then keep your faith, and leave me mine;
All roads that lead to God are good."

MB

12

Of Sex and Self

~~~~~~

Question: I am trying to improve my spiritual self by meditation and perfect Christian living. My husband and I are in our sixties. Yet he believes we should have sexual relations. To me that seems sinful, as we have our family. Wouldn't carrying on like that hinder my spiritual growth? I will abide by your answer.

M. V. W.

Answer: In my study of religions and religious thought, I find little reference to sexual abstinence between a couple to whom love is sacred and the presence of God is real. In your particular case, the sexual act is made spiritual or sinful according to your own point of view.

The sexual relation is as much an extension of honest affection and emotion as a kiss or an embrace. Promiscuity and the thought of guilt in any area may cheapen an otherwise pure relationship, for certainly the desire to love and be loved is in itself a spiritual expression. God is love. No religion has made this more emphatic than Christianity.

It is unfortunate that *sex* has been made a dirty word because of pornographers and the like. If you truly look upon your body as the temple of God, if you are justly proud of being *you,* of your appearance, your health, your vitality—as any spiritually minded person should be—I see no reason why you and your husband should deny yourselves the joy and inspiration of the sexual act.

There are various schools of thought about the value of sexual intercourse. Some medical doctors emphasize the indispensable need for sex as a health factor. Some have even coined the term *sexercise.* Others caution about overindulgence in sex. In Vilcabamba, Ecuador, where Mrs. Bach and I recently conducted research among the long-living people of that particular area, husbands and wives had sexual relations despite their advanced ages of 90 and 100 and even 110. Doctors confirmed the truth of this, and I know of none who insist on totally abstaining from sexual relations, unless there are pathological or illness factors involved.

On the other hand, if you and your husband truly believe, as some ascetics do, that the sublimation of sexual intercourse heightens spiritual consciousness, that is another matter. If you are absolutely convinced that the transmutation of sexual energy will lead you to the mystical, saintly state you desire, that is something you must resolve. Individuals who believe this and who aspire to it usually retire to a convent or a monastery, or at least try not to impose such a highly personal decision on their companions. However, if this aspiration to cosmic proportions is what you feel is God's perfect will and call for you, I can only hope that your husband will either join you in the adventure or say, "Bless you, darling, and let's keep in touch."

Be prepared, if you aspire to this kind of sainthood, to go beyond celibacy into total abstention, a discipline which involves not only mastery of sexual drives but of every other thrust and temptation of the flesh and mind.

Your letter and its candor are appreciated. My only concern is your expressed intention to abide by my answer. This is a greater responsibility than I want to impose on you or me! So love life, love your husband and love God, and every good guidance to you along the way.

MB

Question: Adjustment to one's sexuality poses the same basic problem for the homosexual as for the heterosexual. We "gays" face no basic difference in striving for divine order in our life. We must open every area of our life to God's expression, as must the heterosexual, and no one has proved that a chosen, preferred state of celibacy is harmful. We are not the opposite of a celibate. Many gay Christians are no longer willing to stand apart from the churches in fear.

When human beings are able to place their sexuality, whatever its expression, in true perspective, then this crippling prejudice homosexuals have encountered will vanish.

I do not for one instant relieve the homosexual of the responsibility of acting in tune with divine law in his or her sexual expression. However, the responsibility is the same for all persons.

One of the biggest struggles I face in my life is the elimination of animosity within myself toward so-called "straights" in our society. Truth teachings have been of inestimable value to me in freeing myself from the bonds of resentment and even hate. Surely in a publication of this kind we need not encounter evidence of discrimination against the homosexual. We have no lack of this elsewhere in our daily life.

R. S.

Answer: Not only has animosity against "gays" existed in Western society long before the word *gay* became a colloquialism, but there has been, and is today, open resentment against the right of the homosexual to be treated with the respect accorded the heterosexual. And, by your own admission, you harbor animosity against "straights." We all need to take an inward look.

Your letter suggests a key to introspection and the need for principles that will free us all from the bonds of resentment and self-righteousness. This key is, indeed, Truth, or what I would call *spiritual understanding.* Whatever we term it, the key is the process of a development of mind and an unfoldment of spirit.

When Jesus said, "The kingdom of God is in the midst of you," He did not lay down any sex qualifications. When the scriptures of the world—most of them—imply that the "body is the temple of the living God," there is no express requirement that an individual must therefore be fruitful and multiply, or be celibate, or male or female, or heterosexual or homosexual.

The ultimate admonition is, rather, to recognize one's true state of sex, the sex divine—namely, spiritual being. It will be a great day when we begin reasoning from this point and go on from here!

We have gone into such a tizzy about the word "sex" that its meaning as a simple physiological distinction and its reference to gender have become vulgarisms in the minds of all too many otherwise fairly sensible people. I met a man recently who insisted that the word *sexagenarian* should be used cautiously because of possible misinterpretation! He must have been on the verge of sixty.

We still have a long way to go on the road of truth and understanding, but we are making progress, don't you think?

MB

Question: What do you think of premarital sex?

JUDY V.

Answer: I think that to persons truly in love it is as attractive as postmarital sex. As to the rightness of it, that depends upon the point of view of the individuals involved. Some people have a conscience about it, some a conscience against it. Some indulge in it and their marriages are successful, some do not indulge in it and their marriages are also successful. Some do not indulge in it and their marriages fail. Some indulge in it and their marriages also fail. Some are sorry they did. Some are sorry they didn't. And so on. Make up your own phrases and assumptions and they will fit one case or another.

What do I think? If we are talking about sex relations between a young couple planning to marry and not content to wait until the nuptial night for intercourse, I think they should level with each other on the meaning of life itself. To make sex the central pursuit of marriage is going off on a false scent, to say the least. Love has other equally important aspects besides sex, respect for each other's deepest convictions, the thrill of constructive companionship, the joy of being together, working together, complementing each other, setting up one's own aesthetic and moral standards instead of going along with those of the crowd. These and other central aspects of love are fully as important as sex.

In short, if you plan to get married at all (which is no longer the rule in certain sectors) or if you plan to get married sooner or later, why not get married sooner?

MB

Question: The following is a paragraph from a book which was prepared by a Christian group at a large university:

"Did God make a mistake when He gave sex, when He created us with urgent sexual needs for which there is no satisfactory substitute? These needs can be sublimated and repressed, but this always hurts us emotionally and even physically in nervousness, psychosomatic illnesses, etc. God created us so that we need sexual release, fulfillment and included the pleasure as added incentive to the emotional and physical needs. Our sexual natures cannot be denied and we really give ourselves serious trouble whenever we try to deny it in the inhibited name of morality. Since we are sexual by creation, a person who represses his or her sexual needs is not only inhuman but actually inhuman and immoral, since immorality is actually self-destruction. Whatever destroys self is immoral."

What do you think?

ALMA S.

Answer: I think that this "Christian group" is overdoing its homework on sex and neglecting its studies in the field of "spirit." A great many of their conclusions are hogwash and are formulated or contrived *ipse dixit* with unwitting or deliberate malice of forethought. *Ipsedixitism,* the practice of making assertions that have not been proved and then using them as if they were infallible, has long been a ploy among both Christian and non-Christian groups who pretend to prove the unprovable or twist the arm of truth.

Neither celibate nor gay, neither Christian nor atheist (if there is such a being), neither priest nor psychiatrist has ever proved that sublimation or repression of the sex drive "always hurts us emotionally and even physically." Ask the group if they have ever invited a true yogi to sit in on their discussions. It would also have helped, as far as correcting other obvious generalities, to have had other viewpoints presented.

For the fun of it, read the paragraph again and substitute the word *hunger* for *sex.* Hunger is also an urgent need, but does that mean that it will leave us emotionally and physically depleted if we occasionally miss a meal or go on a fast? Can the hunger drive be sublimated? Let Jesus who, it is said, fasted forty days sit in on the discussion. Did God make a mistake when He gave us hunger?

Or substitute the word *self-preservation* for *sex* and see how this Christian group's line of reasoning works out. Self-preservation seems to be another innate, irresistible drive, yet there are those who have sublimated it in service to other goals, and have even given their lives in love for another or for an ideal. Did God make a mistake when He gave us the urge for self-preservation?

MB

Question: My question deals with homosexuality and sex-alterations. Does the Bible say anything on this subject? Let me give you my view.

Being a lonely woman, and realizing how many of us there are in just the United States alone, has caused me to be greatly disturbed by the increased acceptance of homosexuality and sex-alterations. God created woman to be a companion to men. As it is, women outnumber men, and then for man to upset nature's balance even further by preferring man to woman is, from my viewpoint, worse than adultery. "Gay" guys seem to feel they should be left alone to pursue their way of life. Yet I strongly feel they are as sick as any patient in a mental institution. What is your opinion?

A. R. S.

Answer: Your hypothosis about homosexuals is intriguing. I did not realize that man's affection for man or sex-alterations had reached the point of concern you suggest. Perhaps I haven't been where the action is. I am not condoning either topic in question, but I cannot believe that they are threatening the "balance of nature," any more than polygamy, where it is practiced, upsets the balance in the other direction.

As to sex-alterations: I have been unable to get current statistics on this subject. The only case with which I am familiar is that of an acquaintance who, prior to the sex-change, had been married and had fathered three children.

I do not believe that the answer to your question about maintaining a marriageable balance lies in banning homosexuality or in forbidding sex-changes. The answer is to be found in reestablishing a healthy, happy sense of companionship in male–female relationships, a recognition of the yin–yang equation, an acknowledgment that God did intend man and woman to complement each other in order to propagate human life and discover the bisexual nature of the creative force itself.

How to perfect the married state is, of course, the big question. The solution is not necessarily to be found in more sexual freedom or in more sexual restraint or in more sex education. It is to be found, rather, in a larger view of life, that is, in sex plus love plus respect plus understanding. To appreciate each other and to experience a relationship that is deep and true constitute the high adventure and the challenge of marriage. Nothing less than these idealistic aims will suffice. Sex alone is not sufficient. Which may be why 54 percent of marriages performed in the USA currently end in divorce.

Yes, I am sure that "gay guys" feel they should be left alone to pursue their way of life. And "gay gals" feel that way, too. Whether homosexuals are mentally sick is a question to be answered by the application of the same tests and standards by which anyone is so adjudged.

MB

Question: Do you consider the *Kama Sutra* a pornographic book?
J. I.

Answer: Sorry, no. It is a classical study of the art of love and love-making.

MB

13

Of Religion in Our Time

~~~~~~

Question: How can we get our young people interested in religion? It seems like most of the heads I see in church are either gray or white.

<div align="right">

ELAINE

</div>

Answer: Not only gray or white but also bald or balding—that is what you might say if you were in the balcony looking down on me.

I doubt, however, that hair or the lack of it turns young people off. In my work with students I find that they are continually getting older in spirit, while older people are constantly getting younger at heart. Given time, the generation gap will be a thing of the past.

Young people *are* interested in religion, though they may be bored by its institutionalized expression. They respond to religion wherever they recognize it as an inner, life-changing experience. It does not matter if the experiencer is young or old as long as he or she has the "presence." (We used to refer to it as "charisma" until the word became politically perverted.)

How to get them to church? One way is for churchgoers to demonstrate that the church has something young people want and need. Though there is no guarantee that institutionalized religion will survive in its present form, there are signs that the younger generations *are* returning to those churches which help them gain inner spiritual experience. Witness the Pentecostals. And young adults who are less emotionally oriented are being attracted to innovative services in traditional congregations, and to metaphysical movements in which they sense the inner experience in others and are inspired to find it in themselves. It is not age that matters, but awareness.

MB

Question: There is a type of criticism frequently made against modern religion which is contained in the enclosed clipping, particularly in the sentence reading: "The evil forces of our world would be mightily encouraged if all professing Christians would be caught up in so-called 'spiritual movements' which escape from a world of reality in which the battle for right and justice and peace has never been won by fuzzy sentimentality."

No doubt, modern religious movements are the groups aimed at. How can they explain their lack of interest and their "all's right with the world" attitude toward social concerns and activities generally included in the "social gospel"?

A. D.

Answer: I have received a number of letters like yours since the words you quoted appeared in the syndicated column "News of Religion." In the same column a West Coast minister was also reported to have said that "many spiritual movements of today add up to a mass escape from a world that overwhelms us." You, and many others, ask whether modern metaphysical movements may be among the groups so accused. Let me go into this in some detail because it is interesting and important.

In the early days of my research, some thirty years ago, the Unity School of Christianity, along with most metaphysical movements, became the target for veiled barbs of this kind. These religions groups were accused by the traditional church of being nonsocial, nonmissionary-minded, otherworldly, unrealistic, sentimental, Pollyananish and escapist. The charges went even deeper. Entrenched churchmen and theologians looked upon these "modern cults" (as they called them) as being distorters of scripture, materialistic, self-centered and heretical.

In the light of today's notable defection from historic and institutionalized religion it is interesting that evangelistic critics should have both the time and the audacity to revive old prejudices and resurrect old cliche's.

An historical footnote may well be in order, especially since the tremendous growth and impact of Unity and similar contemporary faiths represent one of the spiritual phenomena of our time. Unity is on the march. Religious Science is growing. "Divine Science" and countless new denominations are on the increase. "Truth work," represented by various metaphysical, mental science and eclectic groups, suggests a religious revival of which the traditional churches are not only startlingly aware, but which is sparking techniques for daily living that ministers of traditional churches are steadily incorporating in their parish ministry. Norman Vincent Peale was an earlier case in point, and you need only pick up the writings of modern, liberal churchmen to realize how they are turning to the basic texts and philosophical insights of today's "Truth teachers."

But to come to your question about an interest and attitude toward social concerns and the social gospel. It was always a point of contention among orthodox clerics that metaphysical groups were not interested in "saving souls." Neither were they considered evangelistic or missionary oriented. Neither were they activistic.

But orthodox criticism was deeper. It insisted that "Truth work" wasn't true. These audacious innovators, they said, had robbed Christ of His saving grace and stripped the Bible of its way of salvation. Furthermore, in those days, it was considered theologically unsound for "cults or sects" to turn to psychological counseling, psychoanalysis and an inward journey instead of admitting to man's inherent sinful nature and getting the sinner right with God through dogma and ritual of the entrenched ecclesiastical system. "Unity," a minister once told me in dead seriousness, "is too happy to be a religion. People don't even cry at Unity funerals."

Most of all, these metaphysical newcomers were accused (as your current quote indicates) of being escapists and deserters from participation in social action.

What the traditional church did not see was the coming of a *new type* of social action and social concern, a mystical approach, if you will, based on a rise in consciousness. This was the mystique which was slow in getting through and which still has a long way to go, but which is inexorably emerging as a spiritual life style based upon the very essence of the teachings and challenges of Christ . . . the awakening, in fact, of the "Christ within."

The old type of social action was precipitated by a century-and-a-half-old concept that religionists should be personally and physically involved in such issues as the abolition of slavery, temperance, prison reform, work reform, political reform and should try to convert the wrongdoers through a conversion experience. When this method did not achieve the expected results, it was decided to boldly bring Jesus into the action and see whether this would not work the miracle. This program sponsored personal involvement on the part of Christian enthusiasts and scholars, and spawned a number of social-action groups, spiritual unions and evangelistic movements.

Throughout all this, while church action became more and more physical, metaphysical movements saw the issues as spiritual and interpreted the remedy as residing in the soul and spirit of man. The idea was to reach the causes and not symptoms. The hoped-for breakthrough was a project in consciousness and a deeply mystical application of the recognition of the God-spirit at work in the world, even to such a degree that the phrase "the Christ in me salutes the Christ in you" became a practical working tool toward effecting a new view of life and a change in situation.

The uninitiated clergyman could not understand this approach, any more than the uninitiated metaphysician could understand the full charismatic power of the Holy Spirit. Both experiences are mystical.

I recall, during World War II, visiting several Trappist monasteries. I asked a young novitiate how he justified his seclusion behind the protecting arm of "Mother Church" while his peers were being killed. "We work in the realm of prayer," he replied. "We believe that our prayers hold the hands of those who hold the guns."

Compared with metaphysical teaching, in which this prayer would be much too literal, this is not a true analogy, but there is a similarity that in both instances a mystical approach is involved and a state of consciousness is implied. Few may like the term *mystical,* but inherent in metaphysical insight is the belief and challenge that that which appears in the phenomenal world is first worked out in the ideal; it is in the spiritual before it reveals itself in the material; it is in the unseen before it makes itself manifest in the seen.

Social action, metaphysically speaking, is an operation in a dimension beyond our commonly accepted four-dimensional, linear-thinking approach, and makes sense only to those who have adventurously engaged in the experience and empirically estimated the results.

MB

Question: The thing I want to know is where in the Bible can I find something that will help me to remember what I read in the Bible? I would like to remember more about the Bible.

A. K.

Answer: Let me offer three suggestions:

1. *Consult a good Bible concordance.* This is a reference book that indexes all important words in the Scriptures. Look up the word *remember.* Then check the texts to which the word refers. Jot down the texts that appeal to you. Think about them. Memorize those you especially like. This will be a wonderful step toward helping you to remember to remember!

2. *Make the Bible contemporary.* People forget what they read because they do not connect what they read about with their own lives. They fail to identify. Become a player in the Biblical drama and you will be able to recall the scenes, the settings and the cast of characters. Imagine that the prophets are living today, that Jesus is walking with you, that the things that happened in the Bible do and can happen to you. Identify! Identify!

3. *Remember what you wish to remember by means of an association of ideas.* Select a passage from the Bible and involve it in as many of your associations as you can. The more you add to whatever you wish to remember, the greater and easier is your retention. Many people believe that the less they have to remember, the easier it is to recall. Not so. The more you give the brain to file in orderly fashion, the more likely the remembrance.

So, build up a series of associations around biblical facts and circumstances. Involve yourself with them as though you had to report on them in detail. Walk the Jericho road mentally in order to remember the parable of the Good Samaritan. Stand on Golgotha in order to recall all the details of Good Friday. Imagine yourself at the open tomb on Easter morning. See yourself in the prophets of old. Listen to Jesus as though you had actually been in his presence (and who is to say that you weren't!).

And by the way, here is an affirmation that may help you as you get into your Bible-reading adventure: *I remember what I read and what I read remembers me.* How could you possibly forget?

MB

Question: A friend of mine tries to tell me that Chinese boxing has spiritual meaning. This sounds like Communistic propaganda to me.

V. J.

Answer: It sounds more like *religious* propaganda to me, but I can understand where your friend got the idea. There are several forms of Chinese boxing techniques which have meditative features, and by a stretch of definition, they could be said to have "spiritual meaning."

One of these boxing methods is *Tai Chi Ch'uan,* basically a series of more than a hundred body rhythms, postures and forms, graceful and flowing through a synthesis of body and mind. This, of course, is a far cry from our prize fights or fisticuffs, or even our most innocent calisthenics. It is, rather, a type of shadowboxing, developed into what might be called "bodily prayer" or, to a degree, "yoga in motion."

The basic principle in *Tai Chi Ch'uan* is that all life consists of, and is set in motion and sustained by, the constant interplay of passive (Yin) and active (Yang) forces. *"Tai Chi,"* say its teachers, "is the root of motion (Yang) which has division, and of stillness (Yin) which has union. *Tai Chi* is this duality in harmonious relationship." *Ch'uan* means *fist* and implies power and control. It also refers to boxing, but, in the Chinese sense, the aim of boxing is total coordination of body, mind and spirit.

Another system, *Pa-Kua* (pronounced "ba-gwa"), is a series of coordinated postures used in developing physical fitness and self-defense. As in the case of *Tai Chi, Pa-Kua* is rooted in the age-old philosophy of the *I Ching,* or *Book of Changes* (1000 B.C.). The art of *Pa-Kua* was perfected by followers of Taoism, a religion founded by the philosopher Lao-tzu in the sixth century B.C. According to my estimate of these two Chinese "martial arts," your friend is right in the assertion that they have spiritual meaning.

MB

Question: Is witchcraft considered to be a religious movement?

K. K.

Answer: It is, if by religion you take the broad view of a way of life institutionalized. Modern witches insist on pointing out old truths, such as the fact that the word *witch* is closely associated with *wit,* or knowledge, and that *devil* is from the root *div,* from which we also get *divine.* Witchcraft has been considered a pagan religion since medieval times and is so construed by most of today's orthodox church people. There are some four hundred covens in the USA. Covens are groups or clutches of ten or more witchy worshipers.

MB

Question: Is there no end to teachers sent us out of India? They come to help us, but it is their own country that needs help. We just got through with Maharishi and now a young man in our neighborhood is getting converts for a new "holy man" who isn't a man, but a boy of fifteen. Have you heard of him, and what do you think of all this?

A. S.

Answer: Since Christian churches have been sending missionaries to the subcontinent and around the world for hundreds of years, it seems only fair that we should be exposed to some of their missionaries.

The newcomer you refer to is no doubt Guru Maharaj Ji, born in 1957, founder and spiritual head of the Divine Light Mission, which claims "millions" of members around the world. Maharaj Ji is said to be the spiritual reincarnation of his father, Shri Hans Maharaj Ji, and to have preached his first sermon at the age of six. He has been traveling for some years now, not only in America, but in other English-speaking countries, conducting "Knowledge Sessions," which claim to teach pure meditative techniques, instructions on how to open the "third eye," how to develop the "celestial ear," and how to awaken the aspirant to the "unspeakable Word of God." Among the disciplines he advocates is an uninterrupted twenty-four-hour period of meditation.

So much for now for Guru Maharaj Ji. Deal patiently with him, Christian, there will be others.

MB

Question: What is known about the history of Jesus of Nazareth, that is, "Jesus the Christ"?

J. B.

Answer: Amazingly little, if by your question you mean references to Him by His contemporaries. Outside of the gospels, scarcely anyone mentions Him. The Jewish historian, Flavius Josephus, makes a brief reference to Him as "the so-called Christ," and Pliny the Younger refers to Him in a short statement about the early Christians. Because of this limited coverage, skeptics have long argued that Jesus Christ may not actually have appeared at all, but believers feel this is precisely how a Messiah would make His appearance—neglected and unrecognized by the world into which He came.

MB

Question: I read in Jeremiah: "I will dash them one against the other, . . . I will not pity or spare or have compassion." This does not sound like a God of love. My heart says this is wrong, but I don't know why. I get depressed when I read the book of Jeremiah.

D. P.

Answer: The prophets of old were insistent that God is a God of law and order. Our challenge is to be trusted with our concept of Him as a God of love. Obviously He is both.

The Bible may be "for all time," but many of its injunctions were specifically for the period and the people to whom the prophets directed their message, and the sooner we learn this, the better off we will be.

Rest easily about Jeremiah. Don't read him for a while. Read about love. Jeremiah started life with an inferiority complex. He had a hard time of it and God had some equally hard jobs for him to do. Bless him and be as patient with him as you must be with me!

MB

Question: I hope I may ask you this without being considered antagonistic to metaphysical movements, but it seems to me that such groups as Unity and Christian Science and others of this kind are too self-centered. I mean, they are more interested in themselves than in saving the world as other churches do. In my church we have missionaries and relief programs and are always helping people whom we never even see. Don't you feel this way and isn't this what Christ really expected His people to do?

MRS. R. B.

Answer: Having grown up in a staunchly missionary-minded church and having been catechized on "as you have done it unto the least of these . . . ye have done it unto me," I am well aware of the sociological and ethical implications of your question. I would even go so far as to confess that during the early years of my research among religions around the world, I often asked myself, "Where are the missionaries of the oncoming Truth movements? Don't they care about others?"

It was only as I became acquainted with the metaphysical movements' philosophy that their nonphysical participation in our standardized conversion efforts became clear and uniquely significant. Understanding the metaphysical approach to what traditional churches call "world service" is not easy or reasonable to anyone who evaluates spiritual expansion in terms of numbers, who measures them by promotional techniques, or who thinks of social service primarily in terms of activism.

To understand the metaphysical philosophy we must enter into an entirely new octave of understanding, one in which the obligation is no less demanding and the dedication no less sincere, but where the means to the end are differently oriented and uniquely spiritualized.

Charles Fillmore put it this way:

> When you recognize an all-caring Father who heeds even the sparrow's fall, you relinquish the idea of your responsibility and you are relieved. Then through the mental freedom which your mind recognizes, there flows to you and to those in whom you are interested greater resources from unlooked for directions. We do not abandon our friends (and fellow beings) and withdraw interest in them, but we recognize their equality with ourselves in the supreme Mind and by that recognition they are freed from a

mental dependency with which we have unconsciously bound them. They then begin to assert their inherent capacities and step forth with the work that the Spirit within them has chosen.

I do not believe this can be grasped without an inner encounter with the mystique involved. I am not even asking you to accept this basic spiritual premise. It is a matter of an adventure in consciousness. To trust Spirit, we must know of its guidance and demonstration by *experience.*

Speaking for Unity at this point, let me repeat something I said in *The Unity Way of Life,* "There is room, it seems to me, in Christendom's rich and teeming family for one movement which thinks of missions in terms of the Word, of evangelism in terms of a stream of prayer and of conversion in terms of the discovery of Self. Among the cavalcade of faiths which pay homage to heritage and tradition, let there be one which respects the constant unfoldment of Truth."

MB

Question: I have just finished reading an article by a college professor whose daughter is a college student who has been brainwashed by the Moon Unification Cult. The group is growing by leaps and bounds and is being financed by big industry. Their appeal is anti-Communist. They are definitely after college students and getting them to drop out. The professor's daughter was completely brainwashed, after having been disgusted at first during two workshops, then completely taken in at the third. We have a center of this movement on our street and their aim is world domination. Any helpful comments?

SHOCKED

Answer: Early in my research on the religious movements of the world, I learned two basic principles. (1) Beware of sweeping generalizations about the merit and demerit of emerging groups. (2) Remember that there are no heretics among groups we might consider heretical. *Heretic* is an objective term. It is used by those who look from the outside in. Those on the inside do not see themselves as heretics or cultists; in fact, they see those on the outside as the real deviants.

In addition to these basic principles, I learned a remarkable truth, namely, that if a movement deserves to live, it will. False, fictitious and self-contrived movements will destroy themselves. I owe this truth to my own research but also to a wise and judicious rabbi named Gamaliel (Acts 5:38–39).

I have had many questions about the Moon movement since its inception. I attended some of the very earliest Sun Myung Moon meetings when this Korean "seer" came to America and in 1965 in Washington, D.C. I was introduced to Mr. Moon and a small group of his devotees. With me were Arthur Ford, the popular psychic, and writer Ruth Montgomery. It was at this meeting that Mr. Moon persuaded Mr. Ford to give him a psychic "reading," a fact that has been much used in the publicity of the Moon movement.

While I have reservations about the ministry and motivation of this presumptuous movement, I must rely on my two principles and my basic truth. What may seem to be "brainwashing" and heresy to an observer unaffiliated with the group-consciousness of a movement, be it political, civic or religious, may be a purportedly useful, workable device for a convert. Such is the reality and the paradox of institutionalization.

Remember Gamaliel, and rest easy. And if, as it sometimes seems, and as the poets say, "Truth forever on the scaffold, wrong forever on the throne," remember that they also say, "Yet that scaffold sways the future, and behind the still unknown, standeth God within the shadows, keeping watch upon His own."

MB

Question: A friend of mine has joined a Japanese religion called Nichiren Shoshu. Someone told me this is a subversive group. Is it, and what does it teach?

N. D. M.

Answer: Nichiren Shoshu is another name for the expanding religion called Soka Gakkai in Japan.

The movement started in 1930, basing its beliefs on the life and teachings of a thirteenth century Buddhist saint, Nichiren. He believed himself to be an incarnation of Buddha, stressed faith in the power of a mandala (mystical symbol) known as the *Gohonson* and used as his basic teaching a Buddhist canonical writing, the *Lotus Sutra.*

Soka Gakkai, which means "Value-creating Association," is a highly evangelistic religion. After World War II it doubled its membership every three years and today claims a world following of twenty million. International headquarters are in Taiseki-ji, Japan, at the base of Mount Fuji. American offices, under the name of Nichiren Shoshu, are located in Santa Monica, California, where there is also an academy designed to train followers in principles promising to lead to happiness and peace.

Whether or not the Nichiren Shoshu-Soka Gakkai movement is "subversive" depends on your point of view. Some people feel that organized religious groups should not get involved in politics as Soka Gakkai does in Japan, having put a dozen or more legislators into office, and that spiritual movements should not have the kind of influence which Soka Gakkai wields over its people through labor union tactics of helping its members get jobs, bargaining for equitable wages and social benefits.

Other charges leveled at Soka Gakkai were based on its anti-Christian stance enumerated in writings called "Shakufuku Kyoten" *(The Book of Purgation).* This criticism against Nichiren Shoshu has mellowed since it established itself (in 1959) as a contemporary religion in the western world.

MB

Question: While visiting in Spokane I was stopped on the street by two hip-type guys who wanted to convert me. They told me I wasn't saved and that they had the only way to salvation. They were Jesus People. What makes them so cocksure they're saved and I'm not, when I really am!

ROLLO S.

Answer: Cocksure Christians are by no means confined to the Jesus People, the Jesus Freaks or the Jesus Army. Every religious movement in history and every evangelist worth his "Praise the Lord!" has claimed exclusive rights on the way of salvation.

I have a hunch that if you or I had been hung-up on drugs or lost in a social limbo, as were many of the Jesus People before they truly found the Christ, and if we had experienced instant rebirth, as some of them have, we might also be standing on the street handing out road maps to salvation.

Columnist Garry Wills recently called the Jesus Freaks "slaphappy and self-hypnotized." I had an opposite reaction. They may be Hallelujah-happy when they do their thing with the old gospel songs and get turned on by steel guitars and tambourines, but in their personal witnessing and testimonials I found them back in the hell-fire-and-damnation days, as hostile as hillbilly preachers toward the seemingly unsaved.

What will happen to the movement? If historical precedent is any guide, it will lapse into a denominational pattern, lose the fervor of its first love and be torn by organizational and personality conflicts. There are already several schisms in the movement. All in all, it will level out and become as un-cocksure as many older denominations are today, even though they too were born of Pentecostal passion and once claimed a tight monopoly on the only road to salvation.

By the way, what makes you so sure you're saved?

MB

Question: What is the address of the Self-Realization Fellowship?
J. O.

Answer: The Self-Realization Fellowship, founded by Paramahansa Yogananda, has its international headquarters in Los Angeles. The address is 3880 San Rafael Avenue, 90065. It has several other temples and ashrams in the southern California area, prominent among which are the Retreat and Hermitage at Encinitas, and the Lake Shrine and Gandhi World Peace Memorial in Pacific Palisades.

MB

14

Of Pets and the Animal Kingdom

~~~~~~~~~~~~~~~~~~~~~~~~~~~~~~~~~~~~~~~

Question: I have a question pertaining to pets. Do you think it is wrong to be sentimental about them? I have never quite recovered from the passing of my little dog, a poodle, who was killed, and some of my friends accuse me of being "paranoid" about this and say a person should not love an animal this much. Is it wrong?

<div align="right">LOUISE</div>

Answer: Your question may pertain to pets, but it also pertains to people. On what fine scale do your friends appraise the weight of your grief? Unless you weep in public or disturb the peace with your sorrow, it really isn't any of their business how you feel about the loss of your poodle.

I lost a schnauzer under the wheels of a speeding car on a Canadian highway one summer, and if the average person had seen me weep at the funeral, where we buried him in a grave lined with balsam boughs and gave him rites fit for a king, I would have been dubbed not paranoid, but *mad.* Is there really anyone who ever lost a pet who hasn't wept? Perhaps.

On the day I write this, the Los Angeles papers are carrying a story about a group of people out here who train and incite dogs to compete in pit fights. They toss two dogs into a pit and watch them tear each other's flesh until one of them dies. They bet on these mastiffs the way people bet on cockfights or bullfights or the death struggle between the mongoose and cobra. There is a great deal of cruelty to animals around the world, and all of this somehow deepens our love and sensitivity for our pets.

So bless your friends and release them. Let them follow the level of their love in their own way. Have one more good cry if you feel like it, and then release your poodle, too, to follow whatever is his "life to come." Say a little prayer of thanks that you had a pet even for a brief time, a pet you loved. If your circumstances allow, why not get another dog? Chances are you will learn to love Poodle Two as much as you did Poodle One!

MB

Question: For a long time now I've wanted to write about a problem that concerns me very much. However, after reading your answer to a question regarding pets and mentioning your little dog, I decided to write you. In that letter you said, "There is a great deal of cruelty to animals around the world." And *that* is the problem.

That is why I find it so disappointing that the meditations and affirmations usually apply only to human beings. I search daily for an affirmation that would decree divine order, health, love, compassion, protection, etc., for all defenseless creatures, but have never yet found one.

Think how an affirmation on behalf of animals might change circumstances for them. For instance, how wonderful if a meditation would read, "God is the reality of all persons and creatures." How can we expect or deserve upliftment and enlightenment for ourselves unless we also strive to uplift the rest of creation. And how better to help our "younger brothers" than by a meditation now and then in their behalf? Oh yes, I can do this on my own and I do, but think what would happen if everybody did!

Mrs. M. J. E.

Answer: I feel as you do about demonstrating our affinity with and for animals through affirmations.

There is very little, if anything, in the words of Jesus or in scriptural accounts admonishing us to be kind to animals, to feel a kinship with them, or to say a prayer or an affirmation for them now and then. Why is this the case? Dr. Albert Schweitzer, one of the world's greatest respecters of animals, explained it when he said, "To the person who is truly ethical, *all* life is sacred, including that which from the human point of view seems lower on the scale."

This is to say that in our reasoning about reverence for life, we should be above even drawing lines of separation among its different manifestations. When we affirm for "people" we should assume the inclusion of "little people" (animals) as part of all people. This may be a mystical approach, but I like to think that the love of Christ which is so explicit in its expression is also implicit in its range of inclusion. The stronger our reverence for animal life, the stronger our reverence for all life, and vice versa. Let's hold this "truth" in a good consciousness.

You might look up in the dictionary for the fun of it, the definitions of both *animal* and *person* and their respective derivatives. Be prepared for a shock and a startling revelation!

MB

Question: Why should we try to find an affirmation on behalf of animal creation? Why not decree our own?

W. E. P.

Answer: Let me select several of the many affirmations and quotations you submitted, and thank you for your research.

"Love all God's creation, love the animals, the plants, love everything and you will come at last to love the whole world with an all-embracing love."—FYODOR DOSTOEVSKI.

"Animals are not brethren, they are not underlings, they are other nations, caught with ourselves in the net of life and time"—HENRY BESTON.

"Nature teaches a beast to know its friends"—WILLIAM SHAKESPEARE.

"The best thing about animals is they don't talk much"—THORNTON WILDER

"Man masters nature, not by force but by understanding"—JACOB BRONOWSKI.

"I think I could turn and live with the animals. They are so placid and self-contained. They do not sweat and whine about their condition. Not one is dissatisfied, not one is demented with the mania of owning things. Not one is disrespectable or unhappy over the whole world"—WALT WHITMAN

"Ask the beasts, and they shall teach thee; the birds of the air, and they shall tell thee; . . . and the fishes of the sea shall declare unto thee. In his hand is the soul of every living thing and the breath of all mankind" (Job 12:7–10 RJV).

MB

Question: I firmly believe that God is love and that God is life. I also believe that God is omnipresent, omniscient, omnipotent and good.

Holding such beliefs, I cannot understand why nature provides death-dealing teeth, fangs, claws, etc., to enable predator animals to kill. And kill they do, and devour other forms of life. God attacking God?

Yet nature also protects or attempts to protect many forms of life from being destroyed by others. Nature provides animals with a sense of smell, sight, running or flying skills, with camouflage, etc. Even in the vegetable world we find poisons (mushrooms) and thorns (cacti) performing a similar service, namely, protection as if for preservation.

How shall we explain it? Can it be that some forms of life are created solely to provide sustenance for others?

H. McB.

Answer: If God is synonymous with nature, as most religions and people believe Him to be, then we must admit that He remains mysterious, holds some closely guarded secrets and occasionally seems to contradict Himself when viewed in the light of our admittedly limited understanding.

If He is in the lemming, fighting its way to the sea only to perish, or in the salmon struggling upstream only to spawn and die, or in the indigo snake which devours its victims alive, full length, without even chewing them, then these and many more aspects of nature may well shock our sensibilities and reduce our sensitivities to the shake of a head and a sigh.

Has the animal kingdom "fallen from grace" along with the rest of us, or inherited "original sin" from *its* first parents, who may also have been living in a paradisiacal garden until they transgressed the law of God?

Deepening insight into the ecological cycle provides as many new questions as old answers. We always had a hunch that all life was intimately related in a delicately balanced system, but we never quite grasped the fact, until recently, that if *we* kill the animals on which other animals feed, we may conceivably destroy ourselves. We suspected that we humans were involved with everything else that lived on planet earth, but it had not dawned on us that, as ornithologist Roger Peterson says, "birds are the litmus paper of civilization," giving us a hint of how secure or insecure our sojourn on planet Earth actually is. Only now do we seem to realize that from the worm which aerates the soil, to the alligator whose water holes save plants and fish in times of drought, we are involved in the living fabric of all life. So we must simply trust God, even where we do not fully comprehend the method or even the reason for His cosmic plan.

According to most scriptures of the world's major religions, the earth was created for man; now we are told that animals could live without us, but we could not live without animals. The birds and the bees got along very well for millions of years without us, but we are warned that we cannot get along without them.

This by no means answers your question as to why there are fangs and claws, or why an ecology of necrology is necessary to keep things going. It is rather well established, however, that animals rarely, if ever, kill for sport. They fight ritualistic battles, they get intensely hot and bothered over love affairs, mating and self-protection, but they are not cold-blooded murderers, nor have they ever legalized war.

"God attacking God" is a tantalizing phrase. It would seem that every life form has its special place and function in the cosmic scheme. From amoeba to man the experience of pain is evident, the innate wish to preserve life is apparent and the intriguing aspect of the mysterious and the unknown is part of life.

It may well be that there are questions on—and off—the quest that cannot be answered conclusively. These the mystics usually resolve by reasoning beyond reason and concluding, as did William Blake, that, "When the doors of perception are cleansed, we will see things as they truly are, infinite."

MB

15

Of Life's Light Touch

Question: Should a Christian think much about sin, or does thinking about it only add to his religious hangups. Do *you* think much about it?

ME

Answer: We can get hung up on obsessive dwelling on sin and sinning, just as we can on too much thinking about righteousness or piety. I am usually too busy to sin, now that I think about it, though your letter impels me to take an inventory! Sin, in my humble judgment, is an awareness of being less than our best and denying God the right of way in our life. It may also, at times, be a necessary encounter on the way to greater spiritual unfoldment.

MB

Question: I have often wondered how you, or anyone, for that matter, can see good in all religions, as you apparently do. Aren't some better than others? And if so, isn't one of them *best* of all?

CURIOUS

Answer: For the fun of it, rephrase your question and in place of *religions,* substitute, in turn, *foods, nationalities,* and *forms of love.* Now what do you think? I'm curious, too.

MB

Question: Do you go to church? If so, where and why?

NOSY

Answer: Yes.
Everywhere.
I'm interested.

MB

Question: I am a Gemini. What color should I wear?

E. E.

Answer: Wear whichever color looks best on you. If, however, you are interested in the color commonly related to the Gemini sign, the color is orange. Esoteric philosophy gives the following correspondences: Aries, red; Taurus, green; Cancer, orange-yellow, also blue; Leo, yellow; Virgo, yellow-green; Libra, pure green; Scorpio, green-blue; Sagittarius, pure blue; Capricorn, blue-violet; Aquarius, pure violet; Pisces, violet-red; Gemini, pure orange.

MB

Question: I have been told that red indicates hostility in auras. Can you tell me what the following colors indicate: gold, gray, green?

C. L. D.

Answer: Auric experts differ in their opinions, but gold is generally construed as the aura of vitality and/or the spiritual nature. Purple and blue are also indications of religious response. Inferences about gray are inconclusive. Some say gray indicates poor health. Green indicates jealousy. Can this be where we get the phrase "green with envy"? I would rather think of "green for growing"—in spirit.

MB

Question: Is it right to joke about the devil? I think we treat him too lightly. Even Pope Paul said he is real, didn't he?

A. R.

Answer: Pope Paul said that the devil is "a living, spirit being, perverted and perverting, mysterious and frightening, dark and disturbing. He really exists and acts with tremendous cunning. He is the secret enemy." But His Holiness was not speaking *ex cathedra,* and consequently the statement is not to be construed as infallible.

As to joking about the devil, that is a matter of your point of view. Perhaps we can "exorcise" him by a proper application of the "light touch." In one old dictionary, it is suggested that, "If you spit on the ground three times, the old devil will have no power over you."

I recall an incident that happened at a men's meeting in the basement (church parlor) of the First Methodist Church in Iowa City. The topic under discussion was, "Should smoking be permitted in the church parlors?" The debate became heated and Dr. Dunnington, the church pastor and a friend of the Unity Movement, was having difficulty keeping the meeting from becoming even hotter because there were those who argued that smoking was the work of the devil.

At this point one of the members with a sly sense of humor rose and said: "This discussion has been going on for some time and I have no idea where it will end. But as I was sitting here listening to the pros and cons, an old Chinese proverb came to mind. Confucius said, 'Many men smoke, but few men chew!' " This was just nonsensical enough to bring down the house. Nothing much was settled about the issue of smoking, but at least law and order and a sense of fellowship were restored, and everyone went home feeling somewhat "exorcised."

MB

Question: Lately, it seems we are all inundated with doomsday predictions, but the one that really has me shook is the group in Illinois who is predicting a cataclysm on May 5, 2000. They had also predicted a massive depression for the 1970s. Would you please comment on this before my neurosis becomes psychosis?

MRS. LAV. C.

Answer: Your light touch assures me that you are handling your neurosis very well and that you are also expecting to be around in A.D. 2000. As for the "massive depression," it looks as if the crystal-gazers have been reading the newspapers, or vice versa. What we establish in consciousness will be established in life, so let's change the trend by a change in thinking. I am always more amazed at what self-styled seers miss than by what they hit. Imagine anyone with half a gift for divining the future failing to predict the energy crisis or the sexual revolution, or that a man from a southern town with 683 inhabitants would become president! The prophets of doom and the apostles of apocalypticism have been around since time began. I predict that we'll survive the amazing 1970s and that May 5, 2000, will dawn bright and clear. Have a good day.

MB

Question: Like all metaphysical students, I consider myself a child of God with the Christ Spirit within. We all think of our bodies as beautiful living temples of God. However, as close as we are to the truth, I believe there is one area where even we only embarrassingly accept ourselves and generally reject and cut ourselves off from others. I am speaking of our body's aroma. I use the word *aroma* because it denotes something pleasant rather than offensive.

Science says each of us has a completely different scent. There is even an advertisement which encourages us females to buy a certain perfume because when put on the skin a chemical reaction takes place and no two women will smell exactly the same.

Perhaps we are too sophisticated and not earthy enough. It would seem that even savages have liking for each other because of the way they smell. I found this paragraph in *National Geographic* regarding the Asmat natives (head-hunters) of New Guinea: "Mourning the husband they shared, widows of Omadesep squirm through Asmot mud. The ritual is intended not only to display anguish, but also to mask (remove) the women's scent from his ghost."

You see, even these natives recognize the individual and earthy aroma each of us have. Not that you should go and throw out your deodorant, but try, rather, to remember you smell sweet as God's child and God made you that way.

HEATHER

Answer: I truly hope your signature is not a put-on, for it carries with it the soft, sweet scent of the heath! And I don't feel that your letter is a put-on, because there are no doubt subtle, hidden worlds of attraction and repulsion in life which we have hardly explored and possibly never imagined. Consider the unknown world of animal instincts, or the fascinating study of sounds unheard by human ears and scents beyond our olfactory capabilities.

If there is anything to your theory, it seems to me that commercial deodorants only foul things up, mask our true selves and throw even our best friends off the scent. Out they go, along with Chanel No. 5 and, by all means, the Aqua Velva man!

MB

Question: Who said, "Everything worthwhile in the world comes from neurotics"? Do you believe it?

T. N.

Answer: French novelist Marcel Proust is your man. "Everything worthwhile in the world comes from neurotics. They alone have founded our religions and composed our masterpieces." Believing it or not depends on definitions and points of view.

As Alfred North Whitehead once observed, "Almost all new ideas have a certain aspect of foolishness when they are first produced."

William James concluded that "First a new theory is attacked as absurd, then it is admitted to be true, but obvious and insignificant, and finally it is seen to be so important that its adversaries claim that they themselves discovered it."

Who's neurotic now?

MB

Question: Can anyone ever know other people as they really are?

E. R. S.

Answer: Not really. We know people by impressions triggered by situations, through conceptions (and misconceptions) based on secondary sources, through intuitive responses and spiritual insight. All judgments or knowledge based on such evidence can be fallible or incomplete. The greater the intimacy, the clearer the view, but also the more unrealistic the opinion. No one knows everything about anyone. That's God's business.

MB

16

Of Peace, Power, and Prosperity

Question: My fellow students who go to a certain church tell me that the Peace Sign is a broken cross. I have looked this up to find the origin but cannot find it. Can you help me?

SUSIE Q.

Answer: Your question prompted a bit of research that led me to an article printed in the British Peace News in June, 1961. The symbol of the broken cross slumbered for many years before reaching the bumper-sticker stage. Writer Gerald Holtom tells us that this sign is the official logo of the London Direct Action Committee Against Nuclear War, and that it is not a broken cross, but a composite form of a semaphore signal for the letters *N* and *D*. *ND* stands for nuclear disarmament.

The central motif depicts a human being in despair, the circle represents the world and the endlessness of Truth, and the open background suggests eternity.

Evolution of the Peace Sign or Peace Symbol:

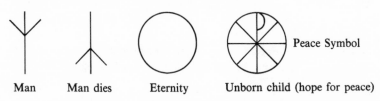

Man   Man dies   Eternity   Unborn child (hope for peace)

Peace Symbol is based on the Chi Rho (Greek letters) a form of which Constantine the Great is said to have seen in the heavens as a luminous cross with words that said, "In this sign shall you conquer."

Peace Cross

The Peace Cross was introduced at the 1967 General Convention of the Episcopal Church. "By surmounting the Peace Symbol with the cross of Christ," said the brochure, "we who wear the Peace Cross pledge to struggle for peace in loyalty to the Prince of Peace."

Credit for the design and its popularization is difficult to establish because it is now used by many activist peace groups. It is commonly attributed to one Eric Austen, whose research in crosses and symbols persuaded him that this particular form usually symbolized gestures of despair and the death of man, but also the unborn child. Thus, the apparent significance of the symbol is that it suggests the predicament in which humanity finds itself in its quest for peace, both within each person and in the world at large.

MB

Question: To settle an argument, weren't most of our presidents Unitarians?

J. and B.

Answer: No. Episcopalians. Here's the record. Episcopalians (10): Washington, Madison, Monroe, William Henry Harrison, Tyler, Taylor, Pierce, Arthur, Franklin Roosevelt and Ford. (Jefferson was originally Episcopalian but became a professed Unitarian.) Presbyterians (6): Jackson, Buchanan, Cleveland, Benjamin Harrison, Wilson, Eisenhower. Unitarians (4): John Adams, John Quincy Adams, Fillmore, Taft. Methodist (4): Polk, Andrew Johnson, Grant, McKinley. Baptists (3): Harding, Truman, Carter. Disciples of Christ (2): Garfield, Lyndon B. Johnson. Dutch Reformed (2): Van Buren, Teddy Roosevelt. Congregationalist (1): Coolidge. Roman Catholic (1): Kennedy. Quakers (2): Hoover, Nixon. Nondenominational (2): Lincoln, Hayes.

MB

Question: What should a true Christian do about Communism?
C. A.

Answer: Be sure that if you try to correct what you consider corrupt conditions, you are strong enough not to be corrupted by the conditions you wish to correct.

MB

Question: An article in the paper said that the churches will be next on the list for the government to examine for income tax purposes and business operations. I stopped tithing long ago because of the fact that religion is big business. Sometimes I felt guilty and I did so when I read the article because I started thinking that if nobody tithed, the churches would have to go into business, because how would they support themselves if all were like me, not tithing? What do you think?

J. J.

Question: An article on tithing stopped me. I used to tithe and nothing happened. I stopped tithing and got along just fine with my money matters. If tithing is a law, then it worked best for me when I let it alone. Shouldn't we do what's best for us? I make no bones about it, I'm in the money game. When the churches need money they come to me, even though I don't go to church. If everything went as well with me as it does in the way of finances, life would be great. In some things I don't get the breaks, but I'm lucky in the money game. And I don't tithe.

O. K.

Question: I find it difficult to understand the law of tithing. What really do we tithe? I am a pensioner with a small bank account. My pension does not even pay my rent, so of course what else I need to cover expenses has to come from the bank account. I have no other money coming in. So please, when do I begin to separate my tenth? In an article on tithing it states, after the business expenses of producing the money has been deducted.

JESSIE B.

Question: I am tired of tithing, tired of hearing about tithing, and tired of being put-on for money. Everybody has a hand out, as if it is part of my Christian duty to give till it hurts. What do you think?

P. L.

Question: I am puzzled regarding the tithing of 10 percent of one's gross income to the church. This dates back to Old Testament days, but at that time the church took care of all giving. The church was the government, as well as the spiritual head of the people. Today when I count up all of my taxes, donations to numerous organizations on behalf of animals (a hobby of mine), and my donations to the church, the total comes close to 50 percent of my gross income.

I do not tithe ten percent of my gross to the church, but feel I am giving generously. Then when I read innumerable articles about tithing 10 percent I feel guilty, but when put in the perspective I stated above, I feel resentful about the attitude of the church in this matter.

In my will the church is well remembered. This I did against my lawyer's advice, who insisted that churches are the richest institutions in the world, and in remembering them I am just helping "big business."

Mrs. W. B. W.

Answer: Every religious act, by its very nature, is the response to an even deeper religious impulse. A tithe, commonly construed as a tenth of one's income, is the outward expression of an inner conviction. An inner longing. Under compunction, or as a sense of duty or obligation, it is not a tithe but a tax.

Even the letter from O. K. sought to prove that nontithing came from an inner conviction, namely, that it was best for him. Now he wishes that everything in his life were as smooth-running and productive as the activities stemming from his apparent Midas touch. Is it possible, O. K., that your self-centeredness about money and your attempt to refute the tithing law may have caused you to be penalized in other areas? Tithing's primary function is not to make money or to "lay up treasures on earth," but to discipline and put in order *total life.*

"As you give, so shall you receive" does not mean in kind, dollar for dollar, but in degree. Tithing produces various blessings other than increased prosperity such as a deepened sense of stewardship in the total circumference of human experience. You will never understand the tithing principle if you define prosperity only in terms of money. The coin of the realm is surely no more than one-tenth of the coin of the kingdom. You can't buy your way into heaven or into happiness, though quipsters insist it is easier to be unhappy with money than uncomfortable without it.

In a culture such as ours, where money is synonymous with power, where we are deeply rooted in a Wall Street world, it is difficult to look beyond this *maya,* this illusion in which success is defined primarily in terms of this world's goods.

Charles Fillmore explained that "the difference between spiritual prosperity and the material idea of prosperity is that spiritual prosperity is founded on an understanding of the inexhaustible, omnipresent substance of Spirit as the source of supply, while the material idea is that the possession of *things* constitutes prosperity."

An emphasis on the possession of *things* creates selfishness and anxiety. Possession of the limitlessness of Spirit creates selflessness and security. You can have all the money in the world and still be poor in spirit. You cannot be rich in spirit without also being prosperous. Tithing or giving in response to an inner motivation, opens the way toward a greater inflow of substance in all of life's relationships.

Jessie B., to answer your question about what we really tithe, ask yourself in what you are rich. Don't forget that there are many kinds of banks. Remember, furthermore, that a widow once put a mite (about an eighth of a penny before inflation) into the church treasury and her act found its way into the most popular book in the world.

J. J.'s report that churches are big business and may be investigated by the government is now an open secret. It is also recognized that although tithing implies the sharing not only of money but of time, talent and other possessions, money is what most religious leaders have in mind when they talk about tithing. "My church members are good Christians only up to their hip pockets," has always been a favorite ministerial complaint. But today, as P. L. indicates, parishioners are becoming more insightful, outspoken and even suspicious as to where the tithing dollars are going and what they are doing for the "kingdom's work."

I used to say facetiously that when I was a young minister I preached tithing so hard to my congregation that I almost began tithing myself. The truth was that my people never tithed because I wasn't tithing, and they were sufficiently perceptive to know such was the case. When I established a "Lord's side of the ledger" and began to tithe, others tithed because of the mystique created by consciousness.

Tithing *is* a mystique, a game one plays as honestly and sincerely as one can with God, or if you wish, with divine law. To repeat, it involves total life. As O. K. said, he is not tithing and believes himself to be successful in the money game, but other parts of his life are in need.

Many churches are prospering too, financially, but they are in need. They are suffering from the same distortion of values, defining prosperity in terms of dollars and cents and playing a managerial role over big business. Defection from the church is apparent when you turn from the dollar sign to the current statistic that less than 30 percent of the people who belong to the traditional church attend its services.

To tithe or not to tithe is up to you. The rules of the game are suggested historically as the investment of a tenth in the promotion and advancement of God's work on earth, but the amount you give, where you give it, how you give it and why you give, from your gross or your net, before or after taxes, by check, by cash, by love or protest, happily or grudgingly, generously or conservatively, are all a matter of your level of consciousness and the insight God has given you to evaluate, investigate and appraise the purpose and the people who make their appeals in His name.

MB

Question: A prominent evangelist, in referring to his friend, a currently powerful government official, said of the latter, "He is a deeply religious man." While I personally do not question the former's veracity or the latter's imputed sincerity, I am aware of the fact that being deeply religious does not necessarily imply espousing the standard of morality that Jesus requires of his followers.

In Jesus' day the Pharisees, scribes and members of the Sanhedrin were undoubtedly deeply religious. Jesus said of them that they "sit on Moses' seat; so practice and observe whatever they tell you, but not what they do." Then He exposed them.

My question is this: Does Jesus assume that being "deeply religious" on the part of a person in authority gives that person carte blanche to political or hierarchal expediency?

D. E. P.

Answer: My answer is *no* if Jesus used the term "deeply religious" —which, of course, He did not.

A second reading of the chapter (Matthew 23) may well suggest an insight into the assumption of what went on in His heart and mind. No doubt He was dismayed and frustrated at the gap between profession and practice in the lives of those in authority during His time.

"Deeply religious," no matter who uses the term, is an ambiguous phrase insofar as the psychology of language is concerned. But the desire to use the phrase is understandable, for every religiously self-conscious person finds it necessary to exalt humankind to God. For this reason it is an awesome phrase and has come down to us through history, muddying the spiritual waters and confounding the mind.

At the time of the Reformation, the Pope, the Emperor and the Reformer were all supposed to be "deeply religious." In the bloody revolutions and counterreformations that followed, contenders on all sides were "deeply religious." The Thirty Years' War, bloodiest of all wars according to some authorities, was a conflict between "deeply religious" Protestants, "deeply religious" Catholics, "deeply religious" Huguenots and "deeply religious" Jesuits. The phrase has persisted from the partition in India involving Hindus, Moslems, Sikhs all the way to the continuing conflict in Ireland between "deeply religious" antagonists.

Perhaps a distinction should be made between "deeply religious" and "deeply spiritual"; but no matter: he who is wise should remove himself from precarious verbal addictions.

The best any reader can do is to open the Bible to chapter 23 of Matthew and decide for oneself what is meant and what the Speaker assumed when He spoke the words.

The best *we* can do, until His spirit is truly recognized as the living spirit in every person, is to see Him in our highest image and interpret Him according to our own current preconceptions of what "deeply religious" implies.

Those who lust for power can easily construe Jesus as a fellow revolutionary. Those who are sensitive to the inexplicable pain and suffering in the world see Him as a man of sorrows, acquainted with grief. Those who find a certain rightness in righteousness see Him marching off to war. To others, He is a pacifist imploring men to put aside their swords. He is the mirror in which His followers have always sought to see and justify themselves. Thus, they have seen Him, not as He is, but as they are. And this is largely true of all of us.

All of these paradoxes are part of Christianity's glory and greatness —and the cause of much of its dilemma.

MB

Question: I have always learned that one reaches success through the door of faith, faith in God, faith in one's innate abilities, and so on. But for some reason or other faith seems to be the most conspicuously lacking element for me in financial matters.

Let me put it this way: I readily accept the attributes of omniscience, omnipresence, and goodness of God. I seem to convince myself to realize His omnipotence in all things but money.

The paradox is that I have made faith work for me in health and in other areas. Also I do always have enough faith to pray about financial situations and to go through the motion of placing the financial problems "lovingly in the hands of the Father."

But despite my willingness to the contrary, I find myself still fretting over finances, as if I doubted God's power to turn things around. I want to believe, but my doubts have kept the solutions away. This sounds crazy, doesn't it? What do you think, and what can one do to remedy the situation?

Desirous to believe

Answer: Your letter is interesting but unclear. Are you entreating for money or for faith? When you place your financial problems "lovingly in the hands of the Father," are you, as you say, simply going through the motion? I sense from your letter that you came into Truth from an orthodox source, and you still feel that money is mammon and God is God and never the twain shall meet. Is this why you have doubts, and can it be this unconscious conflict that "keeps the solutions away"?

To pursue this line of thought, it is possible that you maintain a consciousness of success through faith in God, in man and in your capabilities because your faith in these areas are unhindered and uninhibited by any mental reservations. When you switch to financial matters, however, your faith becomes *ex*trinsic and objective. "Do not be anxious about tomorrow" is in conflict with "How am I going to pay the rent?"

But in the realm of true faith there is no conflict, there is harmony . . . *if* you put things lovingly and trustingly in the hands of the Father in the consciousness that you are truly living as God's child, and if you play the game with God, a game that includes stewardship, tithing, gratitude, a knowledge of God's law. *We must use the values that God uses in order to understand God's use of us and our use of Him.*

Let's make it easy. Develop the same state of consciousness in your financial affairs that you apply in your other relationships. Anyone who is truly "desirous to believe" can make faith work or, better, *permit it* to work in all of life's experiences.

MB

Question: It bothers me the way so-called, self-styled "religious people" are after money. They are no different than people who do not go to church and sometimes worse.

Mia

Answer: Rest easy. Moral values reflect themselves in money values whether people go to church or not.

Belonging to a church does not automatically make a person spiritual, any more than belonging to a country makes him patriotic. Churchgoing is no more a guarantee of character than nonattendance is a sign of depravity.

One's highest (and lowest) view of money is a matter of consciousness and insight. So is one's view of institutionalized religion.

How lucky you are to have nothing worse to be bothered by than the thing that bothers you!

MB

Question: Please explain what is meant by the Widow's Mite. I am a widow and I heard that we are not to tithe and I would like to know.

D. W.

Answer: I wonder where you heard what I have never heard, that widows are not to tithe. That is as surprising as to have someone say that widows should never love!

As a boy in an evangelical home with many ministers in our family relationship, I recall that deacons in our church were admonished to care for the widows and orphans, but if any widow had a mite to tithe, she was certainly urged to do so.

Now, a mite is something mighty small. It is still worth less than half a penny. But to the widow who cast her two mites into the temple treasury it apparently represented all the money she had. The implication in Mark 12:24 and Luke 21:2 is that she gave it as an act of faith, gratitude, adoration and humility. The lovely twist in the story is, of course, that she was serendipitously observed by Jesus.

Tithing is a matter of belief in and obedience to a divine law. It is an adventure in faith. It challenges alike rich and poor, young and old, married and unmarried. It deals not only with money, it deals with life, because our attitude about life fashions the "money world" in which we live.

MB

17

Of Religious Lore and Legend

~~~~~~

Question: What is Jesus' last name?

G. N. B.

Answer: Isn't it interesting that he didn't have one? Family names, or surnames, were not used in his day. It was still the time of "begats," "the son of," "the daughter of," and so on. But then He came and helped to bring it to pass: a more specific identification. Soon we were hearing about Herod the king, Joseph the carpenter, Augustus Caesar, Tiberius Caesar, John the Baptist, Saul of Tarsus.

Had Jesus been born during the years of the Renaissance when surnames came into style, He might have received a family name, but coming when He did and bringing with Him a new calendar and a new age, He brought the name best related to His true parent, God: Jesus Christ. Today, no name is better known on earth and, some would tell us, in heaven, too.

MB

Question: Some say that the Book of Mormon was a plagiarism from a novel of the time. What was the name of the novel, and do you think this is the way the Book of Mormon came into being?

NOT A MORMON

Answer: The novel you refer to was an unfinished story written by Solomon Spaulding about a group of Romans who were the first Europeans to discover America. The title of the novel is *The Manuscript Story.* The Mormon Church emphatically denies the charge of plagiarism, and I believe it could win its case in court. I am, however, not on the jury, nor could I qualify as absolute judge in the matter.

MB

Question: What is the easiest way to figure out when Easter comes in the years ahead?

P. B.

Answer: By far the easiest and simplest way is to look under "Easter" in the *World Almanac.* This will tell you on what date Easter falls each year until A.D. 2100.

The rule about determining the date of Easter was established in A.D. 325. by the Christian Council, meeting at Nicea in Asia Minor. The council decided that the holy day should be observed on the first Sunday following the fourteenth Sunday after the coming of the first full moon whose fourteenth day comes on or after March 21. This full moon is called the Paschal (Passover) Full Moon. To determine *its* date requires an involved tabulation, also outlined in the *World Almanac,* in encyclopedias and in the manuals of High Liturgical churches.

MB

Question: Please explain what "spiritual pride" means. Have asked some church people and no one seems to know.

G. H.

Answer: Of the seven deadly sins—pride, covetousness, lust, anger, gluttony, envy, sloth—pride is listed as the first. Spiritual pride is commonly construed as smugness about one's relationship with God. Usually the expression denotes self-righteousness or a holier-than-thou attitude. This kind of pride often comes, as the saying goes, before a fall, and there is an interesting line in Daniel 4:37 about it: "Those who walk in pride, He is able to abase."

Those who try to make spiritual pride a virtue have a hard time of it because even having a sense of one's spiritual worth is in itself questionable. If we wish to use "spiritual pride" as a commendatory phrase, for example, to describe an attitude of oneness with God, let's use "spiritual consciousness" and retire "spiritual pride" from modern usage. Whatever it means, it is archaic and will get us nowhere.

MB

Question: What are Moslem ministers called? What is the Moslem word for their holy wars?

J. L. M.

Answer: Imam is the term for leaders and teachers in Moslem communities. The use of the word differs somewhat among various Islamic groups, but it is a safe identification.

The Arabic word for a holy war is *jihad.* Moslems point out that the word is often misunderstood by non-Islamic people. They tell me *jihad* refers to those wars in which it was necessary for Islam to defend itself and that it should not be construed as justifying offensive wars. *Jihad,* they say, is a war in which the honor of Allah is defended. *Jihad* may also refer to the battle an individual wages against sin and the devil.

MB

Question: Please comment on the following:

What about calling preachers Reverend, Right Reverend, etc.? Men wear these titles for the purpose of being set apart from other people. They do it even though God condemns the wearing of titles in Matt. 23:8,9.

Preachers in the New Testament were called evangelists, ministers and preachers, never were they called Reverend, Father, etc.

The people who wear these titles will introduce one another as "Reverend" or "Right Reverend" and then speak of our Lord as Jesus and the apostles as Paul, Peter, John, etc., with no title. It is a sin to wear these titles. Remember, in youth we learn, in age we understand.

L. O.

Answer: Your clipping reminded me of something that happened long ago when I worked one summer for the Cleveland (Ohio) Church Federation. The organization was setting up a special series of sermons, and word went out from the main office that only ministers with doctor's degrees should be invited to participate. In those days, I was a young idealist with the passion of the Jesus People, and the decree about degrees really turned me off—and on. I quit the job because of my resentment against this kind of pseudotheological sophistication.

That was part of my youth. Age, as you say, brings understanding, a somewhat different understanding from that portrayed by the pastor whose clipping you sent me. *His* understanding apparently made him more critical; mine made me more tolerant.

I still can't get enthusiastic about the use of titles and degrees. They are often overused and pretentious. But years of research and study have taught me that the customs of our day are radically different from the customs of the days of Jesus. I notice that the pastor had his picture attached to the enclosure. This would hardly have been scriptural either! Would Jesus have used newspapers for advertising His appearances, or would He have resorted to radio and TV or divided the church into various sects, creeds and denominations? But we take these practices for granted. They are part of our time. This does not make them right, but neither does it make them "sinful." Modern innovations do not make our age better than the period in which Jesus walked the earth, they simply make it different. We should consider our time in the light of His spiritual understanding, His moral and ethical teaching, His love, tolerance and goodness, rather than split hairs about semantic inconsequentials and obvious nonessentials.

If God truly condemns the wearing of titles or calling anyone "father," then we have all fallen short of the glory of the Most High. Substituting "Dad" or "Pop" or "Pa" isn't going to save us, and calling ourselves "preacher" or "evangelist" or "minister" instead of "Reverend" or "Bishop" or "Father" will never get us inside the pearly gates.

It would truly be sad if we gave Jesus a D.D. in order to designate His greatness. It would be equally sad if we had to rob others of their well-earned titles—a Dr. Schweitzer or a Dr. Kissinger, for example—in order to discover their truest selves. In youth we learn, in age we understand.

MB

Question: During the holiday season last Christmas a question came to me about the three Magi who followed the star to Bethlehem. Is there any record left by them in their own country as to their journey or any influence shown on their own religion because they saw the Christ? Were there really three? I realize that the common people did not have access to books at that time, but I still am curious.

A. F.

Answer: Gaspar, Melchior and Balthasar! These names given the Three Wise Men have a romantic ring to them. We would all like to know more about their lives and their reports after they returned home.

It seems, however, that the names Gaspar, Melchior and Balthasar are legendary only in Western tradition. In Syrian lore the three are referred to as Larvandad, Harmiadas and Gushnaseph. Other countries honor other names, and it is too bad that the gospel writers did not go into more detail to satisfy the curiosity of us twentieth-century Christians. Didn't they know we would be asking, or didn't they care or hadn't they divined that there would be Christmas crèches all around the world which would include in their cast of characters this remarkable trio of travelers?

There is no non-Biblical record that the Magi went home and reported on either the star or the manger Child. But in the cathedral of Cologne are relics of the three so-called "kings," and their bones are venerated by those who come with a wish and a will to believe. The fact is, the Gospels do not refer to them as "kings" but the term certainly sounds better in a song than to say, "we three *men* of the Orient are."

It is not even verified that there were actually three. It is assumed there were because three gifts are mentioned, but some scholars insist there were twelve Magi, inasmuch as this was a mystical number in esoteric lore. But what would this do to our beautiful hymn if the line read, "We *twelve* kings of Orient are"? Let's stick with three, which is also a mystical number and has a good resonance.

But getting down to your serious question about how they propagated their faith when they returned to Babylon or Persia or wherever they came from, it seems to me that one of the true "miracles" of

Christmas is (and was) the rapid internationalization of the Christmas story. By word of mouth, through missionary journeys, through gossip and travel, the narrative grew and spread, as if by pulsations in the psychosphere, if not by divine design.

Theologically, we return to the number *three.* It is believed that the Three Wise Men symbolically present Jesus to the world as the new Moses, the new Israel and universal wisdom, hopefully pointing to the eternal blueprint of "peace on earth, good will to men" in which all nations and rulers of nations shall one day join.

MB

Question: What is the most popular man's name in the world, John or Paul?

MRS. A. L. C.

Answer: Neither John nor Paul, but Mohammed.

MB

Question: Do you believe that the spirit of God can make people worse as well as better? A friend of mine was always tolerant in his religious views until he had what he called the Baptism of the Holy Spirit. Then he became intolerant, especially with people who hadn't had this baptism, and he turned against us, saying that we were unsaved. He believes that religion must take a hard line and make enemies of people if necessary. So my question is, can the spirit of God make people less friendly than they were before?

P. K.

Answer: I had an aunt who felt she was most religious and definitely on God's side when she was fighting the Catholics. There are people who feel they are best fulfilling God's assignment when they can convert someone to their belief. There are sincere and dedicated people who are convinced that they and they alone know God's will, God's way and God's word, and that their leader came into the world to bring not peace, but a sword of uncompromising righteousness.

These are facts of life, confirmed by religious history, and they are true of Christian and non-Christian alike. Often, the deeper the conviction, the more exclusive the belief and the more self-righteous the conduct.

The Baptism of the Holy Spirit is a controversial subject and a highly charged spiritual experience. It insists that the Third Person of the Trinity (the Paraclete, or Holy Ghost) possesses, dominates and enlightens the one so "baptized," and verifies the experience by a special manifestation. These manifestations are referred to as "gifts" and include visions, prophecies, healing, speaking in tongues, and most certainly a noticeable and usually instantaneous change in life style.

All of this is documented in the Bible and but for this particular baptismal experience, the Christian church might never have developed. Commonly referred to as the "Upper Room," or Pentecostal experience, the story of the baptism can be found in Acts, chapter 2. The "gift" in biblical times was the phenomenon of speaking fluently in a language other than one's own. Today the gift is usually an ability to speak an *unknown* tongue, referred to as *glossolalia.* In this, the language is sometimes a kind of gibberish which is sometimes translated by an interpreter, but is often an unintelligible language in which the baptized speaks to God.

But the greatest gift of the Spirit, as Paul took pains to explain to the church at Corinth, is LOVE, the object of which is, or should be, compassion, gentleness and spiritual understanding.

To answer your question directly: the Spirit of God should always make people better. If not, how can God be good? My suggestion, as far as your relationship with your friend is concerned, is to read Paul's letters, especially 1st Corinthians, chapters 12, 13 and 14. Having done this, find a quiet spot, say a prayer, spend time in unhurried meditation, bless your friend and rest easy—in LOVE.

MB

Question: Do you believe that some day the sun will fall to the earth, as it says in Revelation?

FLORENCE B.

Answer: I do not find any text in the Book of Revelation about the sun falling on the earth, though the quotation comes up now and then in references to the end of the world. Joel 3:15 comes close to it, but not close enough. If you find it in any of the apocalyptic books of the Bible, let me know.

Nonetheless, I see no cause for worry and no justification for a literal interpretation. The Book of Revelation is a symbolic, allegoric, metaphoric account of the struggle and final triumph of the faithful followers of God over the apparent faithless. The account also reflects the challenge to the early Christian movement created by Roman persecution and demands for emperor worship.

The sun has been used as a symbol of God and God's unfailing power. This is as it should be. Largest and nearest of our stars, Old Sol is 93,000,000 miles away. The next nearest star is 300,000 times farther off in space, at 27,900,000,000,000 miles. God's world is a big world. It must be in good hands.

Scientists are not always correct, but they assure us that if all goes well in the future, as it has in the past, the sun will serve the earth for another million years and may serve us all in our energy crises before it runs out of gas (helium, that is). Let's trust it.

MB

Question: What is meant by "speaking in an unknown tongue"? What is it really?

J. I. C.

Answer: It is many things. In Acts 2:1–11 it refers to the mystical experience of speaking in a language previously unknown to the communicator. The descriptive phrase here is "speaking in *other* tongues."

What is it really? It is an outburst of spiritualized rapture, by which I mean spiritual ecstasy. In modern tongue-speaking the language is usually unknown. It sounds as if it were some ancient, archaic language. I would go so far as to suggest that it might, at times, contain portions of original Aramaic, the language of Jesus, and may be psychologically inspired by the overpowering affection which charismatic Christians hold for the Christ. They would call it the action of the Holy Spirit.

The *Wall Street Journal* (May 3, 1976) reported that in the Syrian village of Maalula, Aramaic is still freely spoken today. The Aramaic equivalent of "I am speaking the language of Jesus Christ" is *"hodhe alothat tyiho logtha maher by machikba katinoi babar.*" This sounds remarkably like modern tongue-speaking. It reminds me of a phrase from my own Holy Spirit baptism experience when I suddenly found myself saying, *"Sone machina lanah, jura, lure, manakilira!"* I recorded this in my book, *The Inner Ecstasy,* but have never attempted to have it interpreted. It was, as I recall, a pure exclamation of adoration, and I am willing to let it go at that.

MB

18

Of Psychism and Psychics

~~~~~~

Question: Do you think there are people who hear messages which other people do not hear? I don't mean Joan of Arc and her visions, and I don't mean loony people whose imagination carries them on a sweep of nonsense, but ordinary people like myself.

My husband was dying. The doctor and nurse were on one side of the bed, I on the other. Suddenly I heard three terrible crashes on the roof. Startled, I looked at the doctor and nurse. No reaction. They had heard nothing. A few moments later my husband died.

A short time ago I was wakened by the same three crashes on my door. I thought that our hotel must be on fire and that it was a fireman. I opened the door—not a soul in sight. Then I learned that a favorite cousin in Philadelphia had died.

My third episode is more cheerful. I had a heart attack and was in bed in the hospital. At midnight I was wakened by two crashes on my door. No one came in. Silence—and then I knew I was going to recover. And I did. Would you have an answer or an explanation? I do not believe in reincarnation. I am a strict Episcopalian.

E. G.

Answer: I would put it all down as an interesting experience. Speculate about it and try to assess what is being revealed to you for your highest good. I doubt whether you will be able to figure out these occurrences "scientifically." Certain phenomena in life are beyond scientific measurement for the simple reason that science has no instruments to measure them.

Though parapsychology has opened many doors in the study of the human psyche, and though psychoanalysis has drawn aside several veils that hide the unconscious realms of mind, mystery still surrounds the kind of manifestations which your rational Episcopalian mind insists took place. (And I would be the last to say that it didn't happen as you claim it happened!)

I would, however, like to suggest one possible theory by which to make some sense of your experience, assuming that the sounds you heard were not actually "physical" happenings. There is a graduated scale or spectrum of awareness running from what we consider normal all the way to the supernormal. When we find ourselves in altered states of consciousness due to conditions such as you have mentioned —a dying husband, a loved cousin, personal illness—we are tuned in to manifestations which others do not experience because they are on another part of the spectrum.

This still does not explain the nature or origin of the crashes, but that is secondary. The exteriorization of sensitivity in which the body's nervous energy is projected into a higher or different realm will find its own verification, in a voice, a vision, a sound. What I have called "nervous energy" actually involves the "astral body," but understanding this distinction requires a long and arduous study. For now, let's call it part of the wonderful "mystery of life." I sometimes feel that things inexplicable may merely be a way God has of keeping in touch, while urging us to keep in touch with Him!

MB

Question: Can a person be a professional psychic, that is, a medium, and be normal? Most of those I have met don't seem so to me.

C.

Answer: By "professional" I assume you mean a medium who holds psychic sessions for a price, and by "normal" I assume you mean one who conforms to your standard of morality and conduct. To many people, the very fact of anyone being psychic is abnormal, and to be a psychic is to traffic in abnormality.

The fact is, almost every person is psychic to at least the degree of exercising powers and gaining insights beyond the capacity of the rational mind. Most people have hunches, visions, precognition, prophetic flashes and, occasionally, the sensation of being in communication with a discarnate. Those who claim to be professional psychics have either developed these aptitudes to a high degree through rigorous discipline or innate ability, or else had the gall to commercialize "normal" capabilities or, at times, to fake them.

I have a hunch that the so-called "witch of Endor" (I Samuel 28) was quite normal. The text refers to her as a "woman of Endor," not as a witch. Jesus, too, was highly psychic. How "normal" was He by today's standards? The verdict of modern psychoanalysts is that He needs to be taken seriously. Current researchers look upon Him as a highly accredited sensitive in the psychic field.

MB

Question: We have a daughter, eight, who sees visions and hears voices. Outside of this she is a normal, healthy child. A friend told us to take her to a psychiatrist. Another said we should talk to our minister. Would you be interested in a report on some of these happenings and would you advise us what to do?

MR. and MRS. A. L. C.

Answer: While children who fantasize may, at times, require clinical help, they more often deserve deeper understanding on the part of parents or friends who want to rush them off to psychiatrists. Who knows how much creative, artistic or psychic ability has been molded to fit some norm, or how much sensitivity has been stifled because a child was considered abnormally precocious or frighteningly imaginative?

Some serious researchers believe that a record should be kept of children's fantasizing and even suggest that there may occasionally be telltale signs of recollections of previous incarnation experiences. I am sending you the name of a competent researcher who has done considerable work in this field. You may wish to correspond with him. In the meantime, it seems to me that your assignment should be to maintain a balance between interest, encouragement *and* negativism in reference to your daughter's reports. She may be one of the "New Age" children.

MB

Question: Being aware of the psychic world makes experiences easier for me to cope with, and it is not too difficult to sort out the "real" from the imagined!

I have, with my children, held an open mind, aware of the instinctive faculty as well as the psychic sensitivity. We have very open conversations in respect to both worlds! In this way, fear has been removed from the children's minds. All is taken quite naturally and we approach the psychic as scientifically as possible.

One experience, however, even today causes me thought. I heard Johnnie, about age four at the time, crying in our rear yard. I went to the door and saw him holding a freshly made mud pie over his head, and saying, "Please come down and play with me. I even made you a birthday cake!"

I asked him what he was saying and to whom, as I cuddled him, and he explained: "Jesus won't play today. He always plays with me and we make cakes, but today He won't come down." Difficult though it was to leave this particular door open, I did. Even now, ten years later, I feel that if the child were just imaginative, why wasn't Jesus simply there? Why should Johnnie be so crushed in disappointment, pleading for his guest? Yet, on the other side, it is so much easier to say, "just fantasy."

C. L. K.

Answer: Letters like yours always fill me with the conviction that the more rational the mind, the greater is its competency to deal with what others would call the irrational.

Most of us, and children in particular, live in two worlds at once, and this makes for a greater balance than if we followed those who insist on "one world at a time, please!" As a boy, I, too, saw guides and playmates. Pity the child who doesn't, or the parent who robs the child of dreams that may be more real than fantasy.

Come to think about it, some of these invisible presences are still with me today. Others, I quietly laugh about, and some I am sorry that I let go. If the seen world is the only real world, then the accredited spiritual prophets brought a false message. With no thought of sacrilege, I see no difference between an innocent child poising a mud pie above his head and inviting Jesus to come and see, and a high priest raising the chalice and invoking the presence of the Lord.

Thank you for your sharing.

MB

Question: I am a firm believer in Unity concepts and try my best to live by them, but lately, with the many horrendous news accounts, mass murders, child abuse, etc., it is a Herculean test to "keep the eye single."

Are we burying our heads in the sand, so to speak? Could there possibly be "evil forces" or "powers of darkness" as the Bible mentions, or is it, as Unity teaches, "As within, so without"? Can it simply be mass belief in these seeming powers that is creating havoc in our world?

Will you, with your in-depth approach to such matters, write your thinking about it? I direct choirs of young people and need some definitive answers. Thank you so much!

C. K.

Answer: These "seeming powers" are truly "powers of darkness!" No doubt about it. But they are not evil spirits or fallen angels or the devil and his hosts. They are simply "seeming" powers, *seemed* in consciousness by false convictions, misplaced values, distorted thinking, defeatism, morbidity, by our own mixed-up and often undisciplined selves.

That we are beginning to recognize this fact is one of the truly healthy, hopeful signs of our time. It also represents a metaphysical rediscovery of the philosophy of Jesus, who taught that every person is where he is by the law and nature of his being. He made clear by precept and performance that we hold within ourselves the full capability—and therefore responsibility—over our lives and our world.

The reason people have resisted this teaching for so long is that they instinctively have felt that it might actually be true, and that if they accepted it, they would no longer have anyone to blame but themselves. So they settled for "evil spirits" and "powers of darkness" and the "work of Satan" with a capital *S*, and in the long run blamed it all on God by insisting He could overcome the devil and his hosts if only He would.

Satan is a scapegoat that man created for his own convenience and his own escape from responsibility. The more we personify him, the greater he grows and the more complex our plight.

Check with the young people in your choirs who sing above the din of all this. Some may seek an occasional escape in demonology or in a flirtation or two with exorcism, but their search for meaning is a serious search for Self. The devil, as far as they are concerned, is a symbol only, a "seeming power," and Christ continues to represent a way, a truth and a *light.*

MB

Question: Is it possible for the living to communicate or in any way make contact with the dead?

L. O. A.

Answer: If by the "dead" you mean the discarded decomposed physical form of an individual, the answer is no. If you mean a person's spiritual nature, the cosmic life force, or discarnate consciousness in the sense of consciousness living apart from the body, the answer is yes. The evidence extant in the world's great religions and in the testimony of respected prophets, seers, researchers and accredited witnesses is overwhelmingly on the side of an affirmative answer. This does not, however, rule out the possibility of fraud, deception, self-delusion and a good deal of hocus-pocus in this highly tenuous and controversial field.

MB

Question: What do you think of astrologers, palm readers, clairvoyants, fortunetellers, etc., who say they can foresee your future? I've heard in church all my life that this is sinful and the work of the devil. Yet these people claim it is a gift from God. I'd like your opinion.

JOANN E.

Answer: The categories you mention are all highly specialized and, in essence, scientific, though the early church (and some churches today) would condemn them as heretical. But such churches forget that Jesus Himself demonstrated many psychic abilities and that the Bible is filled with prophecies, "fortunetelling," astrology and parapsychological phenomena.

What do I think of performers in these fields? Just what I think about weather forecasters, stock-market analysts, political experts and pollsters of various kinds. These fields all involve a certain amount of speculation and a need for psychic insight, along with whatever scientific techniques are used in their prognostications.

To repeat: astrology, palmistry, psychism and precognition (fortunetelling, if you wish) are deep, occult sciences. True, there are cheap, commercialized reproductions of the genuine adepts, just as in every field there are those who may willfully defraud, deceive and bedevil the innocent and the credulous. This is why many of these esoteric professions have often been condemned. There is also a good chance that, in areas where psychic forces are involved, "satanic" powers have intruded.

As for the "gift from God" claim: everything, including life itself, may be said to be a "gift from God." It is an easy out to say, "You will know them by their fruits," but the advice is sound and may be a good standard of validity to use in our investigation of these fields.

MB

Question: Would you explain something to me? I have long been interested in metaphysical teachings, which have been a great source of comfort and enlightenment to me. I am also a member of a New Testament church which believes in the primitive concept of the Bible.

The metaphysical concept has given me a different approach to Bible reading and a better understanding of what it means in my personal life. Now, I have read that Jesus was the greatest metaphysician in the world. I have also read recently about the great Indian stigmatist Pio, who had the power of bilocation, appearing to people after his death. I now feel that our Lord Jesus Christ has this power. Is this true?

In all of the contacts He made with His friends after His resurrection, they did not recognize Him until He spoke to them. The Bible says, "He appeared to them" even behind locked doors. There are no details given as to His being anywhere except as He made His appearance to them. Also, did He ascend, or did He disappear? I have some conflicting emotions on this subject. Please straighten me out.

I. K.

Answer: If I am not able to straighten you out, let me at least share in your speculations. Your letter interested me, too, because of your reference to Padre Pio. He was an Italian, not Indian, priest, and I interviewed him in Italy some years ago. It was claimed, as you note, that he could bilocate. He was said to have done so not only after his death, but also during the years he lived as a priest and a stigmatist. People in various parts of the world who knew and loved him reported that he appeared to them in person, but as if in a vision.

There is a good possibility that seeing visions such as seeing the resurrected Christ, may be an inner, subjective experience. It may be a "spiritual sight" that picks up the emanation and triggers the vision.

This possibility would also account for the fact that not everyone sees the vision or recognizes the apparition. For example, I frequently see an aura around a speaker, but many in the audience do not see it. Often others see such an emanation and I do not. Why is it that lovers see things in each other which others miss? A vision may well be a "feeling" materialized, or an emanation crystallized in the eye of the beholder.

Psychic research has relatively few answers to these questions. Why did Bernadette see the Virgin when others did not? Again, why did only a select few see the risen Christ? It must be that there is a strong affinity, a pull as of love or sexual attraction or spiritual consciousness or karmic ties reaching back into time, that cause a synthesis or synchronicity of recognition and awareness. When psychic investigators say that what is seen is not a spirit or an apparition but rather a hallucinatory perceptual encounter, what is their basis of proof? At any rate, there have been too many reports of visions to explain them away as being hallucinatory or hysterical imaginings or merely emotional impressions. We cannot measure with scientific instruments or scientific investigation that which may be beyond science.

Let me "straighten you out" with the suggestion that instead of being emotionally involved with this subject, you make it an area for interesting research and reflection. Because, as in the question whether Jesus ascended or simply disappeared, we are too far removed from the event to know, and too near to current discoveries and insights not to find them excitingly real and challenging, mysterious though they be.

MB

19

Of Death and Dying and Rebirth

~~~~~~

Question: I was told you believe in reincarnation. How can an intelligent man like you do this?

L. L.

Answer: By believing in it not as a scientifically proven fact, but as an important hypothesis worthy of consideration.

MB

Question: I would be interested in your opinion of coma, and how it affects the soul making its transition. One metaphysical treatise says that fear of death causes a psychological panic and that consciousness is lowered through a sense of self-preservation and goes into a coma.

My sister died recently after being in a coma for six weeks. During that six-week period I was torn between praying for her physical healing and letting go and letting God. I felt she was one of the "good guys" and had much to offer in this life. I would be interested in your thoughts on this situation.

WANDA F.

Answer: It has always interested me that the word *coma,* which, in one of its definitions, means "a state of profound insensibility caused by disease," also means "a blur of light from and partly around an image produced by a lens," while, in still another definition, it refers to "the nebulous mass surrounding the nucleus of a comet" (Webster's New International Dictionary, Second Edition).

All of which is by way of saying that definitions are limiting even when they seem expansive. When we say, "She was in a coma," who knows what future research will reveal about her experience? Did your sister sense her coma as a "profound insensibility" or as a hint of "light"?

We may rest assured that whatever the phenomenon, the soul is always above it, or, at least, around it as an image, as certainly as the butterfly is above the seemingly comatose state of the larval caterpillar.

The treatise you refer to *Seth Speaks,* says many things. Author Jane Roberts indicates that the soul does not need to adhere to the laws and principles of physical reality. It does not rely upon perception of physical events as we know them. Neither is the soul bound by what we think of as time. It has its own "time," as it has its own field of perception.

Your ambivalence, whether to pray for a physical healing or for "letting go and letting God," is understandable. We are all caught in situations of this kind. However, there is a paradox in praying which allows ambivalence without doing injury to faith. The paradox is that the "Thy will be done" type of prayer in no way disavows positive praying. Instead, it reflects something deep, basic and Christlike in human nature. The wish and the will inherent in all prayers are conditioned by our level of consciousness, but the ultimate answer to prayer is always in God's jurisdiction.

From the tone and spirit of your letter, I have no doubt that your sister was indeed one of the "good guys," and this being the case, we may expect that she has much to offer in this life even now. Here again we are limited by language and by understanding. We say she "died" or made her "transition" or that she is now in the "world of spirit." But at a deeper level of awareness we sense that her soul is at home in both worlds and that it is only because of our limitations that we speak of these worlds as if they were two instead of one.

MB

Question: One thing has been bothering me for some time. That is, what is the difference between spirit and soul? Jesus said, "What is a man profited if he shall gain the whole world and lose his own soul?" He also said that "God is spirit," and lives in man. I can't break through and understand.

B. J.

Answer: The fact that *soul* and *spirit* are used interchangeably in modern spiritual thought may or may not help answer your question, a question which has persisted since the words were first used in an attempt to understand the mystery of life.

In the days of Aristotle (400 B.C.) the soul was defined as the life principle inherent in all things. In this connotation it was possible to visualize the soul as the deep, animating source of life, and the spirit as a shadow-self which could detach itself from the body to become a figure in our dreams or a ghost.

Certain psychic scholars through the years (and even today) speak of two deaths: the death of the physical body, in which the spirit is released, and the death (or departure) of the spirit, in which the soul is freed.

In an attempt to clarify the inexplicable, think of soul as deepest feeling and of physicality as its manifestation. Spirit is the projection of soul and body in a psychic sense. Interpreted in this way, it would be unreasonable to say, "What does it profit a man if he gains the whole world and lose his own *spirit?*" It would be equally unreal to say that "God is soul and must be worshiped in *soul* and truth."

Think along these lines and you may arrive at that break-through. Modern thinkers tend to think not in terms of body, spirit and soul, but rather in terms of total life as a unitive expression. Together, these entities constitute the integrated self on planet Earth.

In the realm of spirit, after death, the physical body has no relevancy. In the realm of pure thought, spirit, too, is left behind, and the soul reasserts and reestablishes itself as the *cause,* rather than the expression, of life. We might say that God lives in us as spirit, but truly *is us* as soul. I hope this helps!

MB

Question: I am seriously puzzled at the eagerness of so many people wanting and hoping to be reincarnated. I certainly do not want to live again as somebody else. I cannot understand how anyone could want to go through the long, tedious process of becoming a thinking, knowledgeable, understanding human being all over again, repeating the worries, illnesses, and anxieties, to say nothing of the awful hell of losing loved ones and friends. However, many seem to look forward to reincarnation as a "new deal" or the chance to play the game over again with a better hand. I am content with this one earthly life and try to do the best I can. I am a firm believer in the Apostles' Creed, it being in fact my spiritual crutch and walking stick.

J. G.

Answer: Let's look at it this way: if there is anything to reincarnation, we *have* lived before and gone through everything you say you would not want to experience again. If this *is* true, evidently we do not have much to say in the matter. Does a butterfly know it was once a caterpillar, or does a caterpillar remember its butterfly background? Could either do anything about it if it did remember?

It isn't really so bad, is it, this experience of living in physicality, this high adventure of awareness, this thrilling quest for meaning, this participating for a while in the mystery and unfinished wonder of our whirling world?

The "awful hell," as you call it, of losing loved ones, can be offset by the heavenly awe of standing thoughtfully in the midst of death and believing in life. These responses are based on states of mind and levels of consciousness. Each person eventually works these responses out according to his or her wish and will.

Those who embrace the doctrine of reincarnation seem to find great hope in it. They say: "To one that is born, death is certain; and birth is certain to one that has died. Therefore, the whole thing being unavoidable, why should we fear?"

At all events, if we had never *been* we would never have *known.* We cannot experience life if we have not lived, and we cannot experience reincarnation unless we have been reincarnated. But the mystery and wonder of it all is that even if we have experienced it, we still know nothing about the experience.

This may not seem to be the way it should be, but this is the way it is.

MB

Question: What is meant by the term "the silver cord," and what are we to learn from the phrase, "whene'er the silver cord shall break"?

V. W.

Answer: One of the most meaningful interpretations of the phrase is the belief that the vital body (mind and spirit) and the merely physical body are united by a slender, silvery, gossamer cord which is not severed until death has fulfilled its mission. Death's mission, according to occultism, psychism and some philosophical interpretations, includes: a review of the past life by the mind and physical body, a preview of the life to come, and the spiral motion of the vital body departing from the gross body, taking with it the soul. Death's breaking point is referred to as the breaking of the silver cord. Half of the cord remains with the dense body and the other half ascends with the vital or higher body.

It is believed by many students of the esoteric and the occult that the breaking of the silver cord has actually been seen by people with "psychic sight." They also believe that any interference with a "natural death," such as medication, undue lamentation by friends and even cremation or burial before an appropriate time (usually three days) hinders the proper "breaking" of the cord.

MB

Question: Jesus says in the Bible, "Before Abraham was, I was," and at another time Jesus says that He will come back again. Is this not a proof that He believed in reincarnation?

H. F. H.

Answer: The text you quote (John 8:58) is one of the standard passages used to support the doctrine of reincarnation. I think it, along with others such as Matt. 18:13–16, suggests a strong case for the reincarnation theory. It should be pointed out, however, that in the Revised Standard Version and the King James Version of the Bible, as well as in many other translations, the text is, "Before Abraham was, I am." Possibly you misquoted the text of the American Standard Version: "Before Abraham was born, I was."

As to the "Second Coming," it must be remembered that the majority of apocalyptic scholars in traditional religion insist that this manifestation will not occur by way of another incarnation but by the actual descent of Jesus Christ from the heavens, even as He was once believed to have ascended.

MB

Question: Two college students were caught in a sleet storm driving home for the holidays. There was an accident. Bob, driver of the car, was killed. Jack was not hurt. Jack told me after Bob's funeral that they had both prayed that they would get through the storm safely. Why weren't they both spared or both killed?

L. B.

Answer: The easiest answer and perhaps the best would be to say that "God only knows." There is a theory, however, that there are laws to which God Himself is bound: universal laws, cosmic laws, Nature's laws. Try to think through the circumstances of the accident —and life—in this light and see what you come up with.

Let's remember, too, that happenings which are currently unanswerable may at some future period be understood. We apparently do "see things through a glass darkly," but we should also remain open to the possibility that some day a clearer perception will come through.

MB

Question: Could you help me give my twelve-year-old son an answer to the question he asked me? My father-in-law took his life last week. He was truly a wonderful man. His only child, my husband, died eight years ago at age thirty-six. My son, who was then four and a half, can't remember him, but he did love his grandpa.

He said to me: "Mom, Grandpa didn't smoke, drink, cuss or hurt anyone. He always went to church. Why didn't God help him get well?"

B. H.

Answer: Try to explain to your son that every person has deep-seated concerns, and meets challenges, and often irresolvable situations which no one else can fully comprehend. No one really knows what Grandpa went through or on what basis he made his decision.

A twelve-year-old may not understand such things as psychopathological conditions created by diseases of body and mind, or loss of the will to live due to complete spiritual depletion. But he will understand that great and lovely souls, in moments beyond comprehension, have given up or given in to a wish to die. There are some twenty-six thousand suicides in the United States each year—a rate of about twelve per one hundred thousand population. Life is to be lived and suicide is not to be condoned, but each case must be interpreted in the light of our limited knowledge of the reasons behind the act.

I would try quietly to correct your son's impression that "God let Grandpa do this," or that "God did not help him," or that, because his grandfather was highly moral and dedicated to his church, this could not and should not have happened. God is not made in our image, nor can we possibly dictate what He should have done. Since He is life, love and truth in action, His view is far above our knowing and presents a strong motivation to increase our spiritual understanding, our trust and our belief that meaning will unfold as we mature and grow in faith and insight into life.

Most helpful of all to your son is your sensitivity, so beautifully evident in your letter, your obvious love and admiration for Grandpa's life and your concern to transmit these qualities to your son. After all, it is not so much what you *say*, it is what you are and what he sees in you that will truly influence him and shape his thinking.

MB

Question: A matter of much thought for me has been the "eternal damnation and torment of the lost soul." Your views of this subject would be welcomed and appreciated.

S. H. B.

Answer: I need to think about this some more, but at present it seems inconceivable and preposterous to postulate a God who would damn what He has created and torment what He had made! Don't you think so?

MB

20

Of the Search for God

~~~~~~~~~~~~~~~~~~~~~~~~~~~~~~~~~~~

Question: What is God? As a child I was taught that God was a man in heaven (the sky) who knew everything and answered all prayers. In my late teens and for several years thereafter, I thought I was an atheist. I say "thought" because I never stopped praying—just in case. Later I realized I did believe. I knew my prayers were being answered. I knew there was a God who answered my prayers, but what form does this God take?

When I asked Christian friends, "What is God?" I got varied and vague answers. Many people prefer to talk about "The Supreme Being" or "The Ultimate Good" or other such euphemisms. People often don't like to use the word *God.* It embarrasses them. So I don't ask anymore. I can't find the answer in books. I am looking for a down-to-earth, easy-to-understand answer to my question.

S. Q.

Answer: The form of God, the nature of God, the appearance of God, a convincing definition of God—all have eluded priests, prophets, poets, philosophers and painters since the beginning of time. Even the great spiritual messengers left us without a direct and simple answer. God is too big for definition and that is what makes Him what He is.

Yet, when we stop looking for an *answer* and are willing to settle for an *awareness,* a *knowing* and a *feeling,* the problem becomes simpler.

Find a quiet spot in the great outdoors. a place where you can hear only the sounds of nature. Calmly take a deep breath and say to yourself, "Thank You God!" You will then perceive Him.

Drop into an empty church (which should not be difficult), sit or kneel, close your eyes and tell yourself that "God is a Spirit and they that worship Him shall worship Him in Spirit and in Truth."

Next time you are jostled in city streets or caught in city traffic or enmeshed as, at times, most of us are, by the world of people and sounds and motion, repeat deeply and sincerely to yourself, "There is but one Presence and one Power in the universe, God the Good, Omnipotent."

In your confrontation with the mystery of life in moments of joy and sorrow, force yourself to affirm, "I know, and, God, I know that You know."

In each case, you will have your awareness, your knowing and it will be yours, all yours. Why ask others? Why be concerned with euphemisms? Why bother about those who don't like the word *God?* Let them follow their own questing. Jesus called Him "Father" and let it go at that. He thought of Him as Love, as if to say, "That's good enough for me."

I am overwhelmed when I think of God holding countless speeding galaxies in His hand, juggling planets and stars and all the other myriad entities of the whirling worlds, while keeping me balanced on a tilted spinning spaceship, Earth. But how simple He really is when I see Him in a flower or catch His shadow as He blesses me with just another breath of life.

Good questing!

MB

Question: What is the oldest and what is the largest religion in the world?

TERRI

Answer: The oldest: Animism. It is not classified as an institution-alized faith. It is a belief that "spirits" animate inanimate and animate things alike. The largest: Christianity. There are more professed Christians than there are members of any other single movement,

1,000,000,000. But, as a whole, there are more non-Christians than there are Christians, 1,600,000,000.

MB

Question: In one of your talks you gave definitions of religion by various philosophers. Do you remember these after quite a number of years, or can you tell me where to find this information?

A. J. A.

Answer: Let me share with you several of these interpretations as I remember them.

Kant: "Religion consists in our recognition of all our duties as divine commandments."

Hegel: "Religion is the knowledge acquired by the finite spirit of its essence as Absolute Spirit."

Descartes: "Religion consists of the certainty that God exists and that He has implanted in me the concept of a perfect being which, though I do not fully represent, I can think about and envision."

William James: "Religion consists in the perception of the Infinite under such manifestations as are able to influence the moral character of man."

Rudolph Eucken: "Religion is a mystical experience in which the oppositions of life are transcended."

All of these definitions are interesting, but perhaps more interesting would be your own definition of what religion means to you.

MB

Question: Is there any church that teaches a doctrine of happiness? What I mean is, religions are always stressing love, love, love, or salvation, salvation, salvation, or some such. Isn't there a church that goes all out for just being happy?

J. J. K.

Answer: Have you checked on the metaphysical groups? I was under the impression that metaphysical groups are "all out" to dispel the gloom and morbidity of the old-time religion and that they feel that happiness and love or even happiness and salvation are not incompatible.

Perhaps we need your definition of "happiness." Someone once said that happiness is a mystery, like religion, and should never be rationalized. Columnist Eric Hofer once said, "The search for happiness is one of the chief sources of unhappiness."

In ancient Greece a movement called Cyrenaics had an impressive heyday. It was started by Aristippus of Cyrene, and its doctrine was that the most spiritual life was the one that contained the most pleasure and the least pain. Some referred to it as a hedonistic movement, but Aristippus didn't like this because it implied that pleasure is the main source of happiness. He preferred the word *eudaemonistic,* which means that there is a spirit of true happiness (spiritual happiness) in every person and that this reveals itself best through honest living with oneself and one's fellow humans. That kind of "church" is no doubt nearer than we think, in the heart and soul of each of us.

MB

Question: Our minister is always referring to God as the "Great Unmoved Mover." When I asked him where he got that term he said he didn't know. Who said it?

Mrs. E. R.

Answer: Aristotle.

MB

Question: Being a lifelong member of a strict denomination I cannot always agree with you, but for that matter, I no longer agree with my own church, and am wondering where to go or just where I stand. That would be my question.

E. L. T.

Answer: Take a church break. Go to a service other than your own for a change. An investigation of the other person's faith will give you a new insight into your own faith. Or you may even be led into new paths of righteousness for His name's sake.

MB

Question: I have been a Truth student for over thirty years, so my questions are not based on arguments or contention but as a sincere seeker.

I have several questions. In the Living Bible, Ps. 144:4: "Why bother at all with the human race? For man is but for a breath." And Ps. 146:4: "For every man must die." If man's time is so fleeting, why are we put through these paces, suffering and dying, feelings of despair and desolation, disease and catastrophe? It's a big price for just being!

Also, how do you reconcile the vengeance and hate of the God-fearing people of the Old Testament to the doctrine of "return good for evil, pray for them that despitefully use you, love one another," and so on.

My long life has been spent mostly in the service for others, not asking or expecting anything in return, but lately I have had my doubts as to whether anything good will come of all this—universally, that is.

D. J. G.

Answer: Sometimes I wish they had let the King James Version of the Bible stand as is—or as it once was—though it, too, went through various revisions after its first issuance in 1604. The numerous modern translations all lean more and more toward colloquialisms.

The first text you quote (Ps. 144:4) is certainly more understandable and more descriptive in the King James version, where it reads, "Man is like to vanity, his days are as a shadow that passeth away." And Ps. 146:4, "For every man must die!" is found in the King James Version as, "His breath goeth forth, he returneth to his earth."

All Scripture, as has been said, is given for inspiration and instruction. Let me add that it is given for an expansion of consciousness, and this is where art, beauty and imagination come in, because consciousness is enriched by metaphor, stirred by poetry, and enhanced by grand impulses of creative thought.

Literal translations are simply too confining, too narrow, for us to catch the cosmic grandeur of those Biblical writers who tried to "think God's thoughts after Him." This is where the seer, the psychic and the dreamer come in. This difference is especially true of the Psalms, those etheric poems which sang in the heart of the wandering Jew. This is why the Psalms were sung and chanted in the liturgical churches, as they were in the synagogues, and as they continue to echo in the human heart. True, they speak of death, but it is always with the touch of everlasting life with God. Well, you know all that. You know that time *is* fleeting, but suffering and death are only the passing shadows enfolding joy and life. Despair and desolation are merely steps to light and love along the way of faith.

The transition from a God of vengeance and hate to a God of fatherly compassion is part of the phenomenon of the coming of Christ and His realization in the hearts of individuals. "The Christ in me salutes the Christ in you" gives God Himself a new salutation within humanity.

It is all rather wonderful, and even when, as you say, we have our doubts that service to others always "pays off" or that "anything good will come of our efforts," something deeper than our seemingly rational mind tells us that all is well, something beyond doubt assures us these are our Psalms we are singing, and possibly we have already sung them premortally many times before.

MB

Question: What is the difference between a man being spiritual and a man being religious?

J. F.

Answer: The difference between a man being religious and a man being spiritual may be comparable to a man being affectionate and a man being loving. *Religious* suggests a formal, proper, sectarian, studied approach to God and life, an affection which can be quite wholesome and sincere. *Spiritual* carries the connotation of love in action, warmth, insight, a touch of the mystical. The implication of religiosity is that of mere affection or pretense of religion. Spirituality is interpreted as spiritual-mindedness. It is more significant and complimentary these days to be referred to as a *spiritually* oriented person than a *religiously* oriented individual.

But, either way, the good life comes not by definition but by what we do and are along the pathway of the quest.

MB